Previous Praise
for Don Miller

"The 1956 basketball state champions—Carr Creek High—
builds upon a tradition that was started with the team of
1928. When you read about what they accomplished . . . it
shall make all Kentuckians proud."

—BRERETON JONES, former Governor of Kentucky

OVERTIME KIDS

OVERTIME KIDS

The Untold Story of a
Small-Town Kentucky
Basketball Team's
Unlikely Rise to the
State Championship

DON MILLER, ED.D.

TURNER

Turner Publishing Company

445 Park Avenue • 9th Floor
New York, NY 10022

200 4th Avenue North • Suite 950
Nashville, Tennessee 37219

www.turnerpublishing.com

*Overtime Kids: The Untold Story of a Small-Town Kentucky Basketball Team's
Unlikely Rise to the State Championship*

*Another edition of this book was published as
The Overtime Kids: Carr Creek High: 1956 Kentucky State Champions*

This publication was produced using available material. The publisher and
author regret they cannot assume liability for errors or omissions.

Cover design by Mike Penticost

Library of Congress Cataloging-in-Publication Data

Miller, Don.
 Overtime kids : the untold story of a small-town Kentucky basketball team's
unlikely rise to the state championship / Don Miller.
    p. cm.
 Originally published: Paducah, Ky : Turner Pub. Co., c2001.
 Includes index.
 ISBN 978-1-59652-822-2
 1. Carr Creek Community Center High School (Carr Creek, Ky.)--Basketball-
-History. 2. Basketball--Kentucky--History.
 GV885.43.C38M573 2011
 796.323'6209769165--dc22

2011005167

Printed in the United States of America
11 12 13 14 15 16 17—0 9 8 7 6 5 4 3 2 1

To Morton and Dale Combs and their children—Glen, Susan, and in loving memory of son, Len Combs.

Contents

Acknowledgments

In writing a book, it is helpful and often necessary to have the support of many people. I received that.

I would sincerely like to thank the following people for their endless encouragement and "war stories" during my research and for supplying "personal pictures or written information: Bobby "Bob" Shepherd, E. A. Couch, Warren G. Amburgey, Freddie Maggard (came to our home for a long interview and supplied pictures), Ed Richardson, Marcus Combs (sent a self-profile and family pictures), Ray Stamper, Estill Adams, Donald Guy Combs, Donald Hylton, Glen Combs, and Richard "Rick" Johnson. A note of special appreciation to guard, Jim Calhoun, for materials and pictures of the 1956 team, as well as for being available to answer our questions. "He is a keeper of the flame for his team."

To the coaches, Morton Combs and his capable assistant, Willard "Sprout" Johnson, for their invaluable remembrances and joy for the project.

A heartfelt note of gratitude for Beulah Mae Mullins Ashley for sending a profile and picture of her brother, John C. Mullins–the only deceased ball player that played on the Championship Team.

To Margaret Lynn Amburgey (Patton)—we have total admiration for your "spunk" and "zest for living." Thank you for sharing family photographs.

To Blanche Hylton Maggard (Robertson) for being available when we needed a name "for a specific" and sharing an early photograph of son, Freddie.

To Howard McCann, Carr Creek's newest friend, for his enthusiastic support of this project. He supplied a brief profile, pictures, and a video of his family and himself enjoying their first visit to "Carr Creek Hill."

Many thanks and much love to the following for their information on cheerleading and the social environment on the "Carr Creek Hill" during their school years: Ann Kathleen Johnson Pratt, Susan Combs Hammack, Imogene Francis Watts Tyler, Jacqueline Mae "Jackie" Watts Kelly, Ivetta Reedy Washko, Sharon Dale Watts Longacre, Betty Adams Stamper, Sue Watts Adams, and a very special thank-you to our five 1956 cheerleaders for their personal information and insights to their personalities: Jane Carolyn Calhoun Couch, Peggy Lynn Collins Hopper, Polly Geraldine

Mullins Merritt, Nora Jean Hamilton Bentley, and Christine Reedy Godsey. They certainly have our respect.

Some of these "informants" were four-year cheerleaders and all were cheerleaders for their beloved Indians. The informants supplied us with keen insights to the personalities of the Champions.

Much appreciation to owner-managers Orgus and Ruth Seals of the Quiltmaker Inn, Main Street, Hindman, Kentucky, for letting us use their most unique antique hotel as our own for interviews of Creekers—Nora Jean Hamilton Bentley, Warren G. Amburgey with brother Jesse Lee Amburgey, and Rudean Adams, interviewing for his recently deceased father, Sidney Adams, a former school-bus driver and Kentucky State Representative.

Absolute thanks to Nelle Hays Johnson for her continuing encouragement and for her flawless memory. She "coached" a nonwriter in this project.

A special note of appreciation and my heartfelt love to Dale Smith Combs, my teacher in English and General Business. She is our beloved Mrs. Combs, and I am grateful for her continuing quiet way of encouraging and offering asked-for advice. Her memory came to my rescue more than once. She lived it and drove basketball players home after practice or games to prevent tired players from walking great distances. She was "the main support system" for Coach Morton Combs. She was the teacher, guidance director, and mom to star basketball player Glen Courtney and four-year cheerleader Susan Combs.

Sue and I owe our typist, Bonnie Bowlin, a big thank-you for the amount of time she gave us in a very difficult assignment. She has done a fantastic job.

—*Don and Sue Watts Miller*

Introduction

Many people feel that it was deserved justice for Carr Creek High School to finally win the 1956 State Basketball Championship in Memorial Coliseum in Lexington. All the 1956 players knew about the Carr Creek legacy–going back to the 1928 basketball team that finished second after playing Ashland High School to four overtime periods and ended up losing to the much larger high school by 13–11.

Many people do not know that Carr Creek High School was in the 1930 Kentucky State Basketball Tournament and beat Moreland High School 19–15 in the first round. They lost to Corinth 17–11 in the quarter finals. Many of the same players on the 1928 team were still playing on the 1930 team. Of course, all Kentucky high school basketball fans know that Carr Creek went to the National High School Championship games on the campus of the University of Chicago and won three games and eliminated the favorite of the National Tournament, Austin, Texas High School.

The fans in Chicago were very disappointed that Carr Creek failed to make it back in 1930. The 1928 Carr Creek showing in the Nationals raised the hopes of other small mountain schools to emphasize their teams. And it paid off. Hazard won the Kentucky State Basketball Championship in 1932. (Morton Combs, the coach of the Carr Creek 1956 champions, scored the winning goal for Hazard.) Corbin High School won in 1936; tiny Midway High School won the state championship in 1937; another small school, Sharpe High School won in 1938; Brooksville High School won it all in 1939. (My uncle, Herman Hale, was the coach.) Hazel Green Academy won in 1943; Harlan, with Wallace Clayton "Wah Wah" Jones, captured the title in 1944. Hazard again in 1955. And the "Overtime Kids" of Carr Creek in 1956.

It was 16 years before Carr Creek returned to the state tournament. The 1948 team made a good run for the state tournament. They beat Fort Knox High School 52–45. In the second round, the Creekers beat Covington Holmes 57–53. Holmes was the largest school in the tournament with more than 2,000 students. In 1948, there were around 50 boys in attendance at Carr Creek. In the semifinal game, Maysville beat Carr Creek in an overtime period 56–54. Carr Creek defeated Louisville Male in the consolation game for third place. Don Miller and Bill Morton made the all-tournament team.

Though Carr Creek maintained good teams each year, it was the 1956 team that won it all. Morton Combs was the head coach and was assisted by Willard "Sprout" Johnson. Players on the state tournament team were E. A. Couch, Warren G. Amburgey, Bobby Shepherd, Marcus Combs, Freddie Maggard, John C. Mullins, Estill Adams, Jim Calhoun, Ed Richardson, and Ray Stamper; managers were Donald Hylton and Donald Combs; mascots were Glen Combs and Richard "Rickie" Johnson. We are going back and taking a look at the coaches, players, cheerleaders, and managers, as well as the mascots and others who played a role in the success of the team.

A drive throughout Knott County will give you some idea why Carr Creek keeps bringing up good players year after year. You will see basketball goals, of all sorts, barrel hoops, bottomless buckets and the like, especially those nailed to barn doors. Summer or winter, rain or shine, boys of all ages dribble lopsided balls over the cow tracks and fire shot after shot at the goals. (I was so young that I don't remember shooting my first basketball. I do remember that we used a sock rounded within a sock and shooting at a bottomless five-pound lard bucket. After all, there wasn't anything else to do. Also, our parents didn't mind because it kept us busy and out of trouble. This type of recreation is not anything new. The same can be said about the 1928, 1948, and 1956 players who made this practice worthwhile, and it culminated into a state championship.)

The school itself is one of the many examples of how

mountain communities banded together to help the children in getting an education, and basketball has provided a college education for scores of student athletes from the small school.

Until 1920, there was no school near Carr Creek. Then a group of residents got together and organized the Carr Creek Community Center. The residents of the hollows sent circulars asking for small donations to get the school started. The Daughters of the American Revolution and the War of 1812 took an interest.

A one-room school with 26 students opened that fall. Later, as donations came in, other buildings and quarters for boarding students were erected. No student able to pay was accepted as a boarder. Boarding students were kept until 1946. (I was a part-time boarding student during the 1944-1946 school years.)

The Kentucky State High School Basketball Tournament is a "happening." People see each other there whom they normally do not see for the rest of the year. I had the honor of playing in this event in 1948. Though I played at Morehead State College from 1948 to 1952, it was the Kentucky State Tournament that thrilled me the most. The following is an example of this from a book by Earl Cox, noted sportswriter of Kentucky:

"This book is dedicated to everyone who loves the Kentucky State Basketball Tournament, and to all the players, the coaches, the officials, and administrators who have made the 'Sweet Sixteen' unique. Our 16-team tournament is one of the few things that bring Kentucky people together. People come from all 120 of our counties.

"People who should be thanked, but there are so many. Surely, Morton Combs must be mentioned. This soft-spoken gentleman, who has been so involved in the tournament's history, organized Knott County people who raised money to sponsor two state champions that no longer have schools—Hindman and Carr Creek.

"Combs played for Hazard and his basket gave the bulldogs a victory over Louisville Male High and the state championship in 1932. In 1956, Combs coached Carr Creek to the state championship."

This small high school has also excelled in the academic arena, going back to the 1927 and 1928 teams.

Most of the 1956 team members were a copy of the 1948 team and other teams in between in that the majority of the players were coal miners' sons. Therefore, we came from the same socioeconomic background, so there was not much jealousy because very few of us had cars. Our dads worked extremely hard in a dangerous, dirty workplace. Most of the coal miners who worked for years usually suffered some kind of physical damage. There were far too many deaths. They loaded coal with a shovel in the most claustrophobic surroundings possible. The top of the mine was called slate. It could fall and kill multiple miners in one fall. Yet those gallant men were extremely proud to mine the coal and help keep others warm. My father was lucky. After working 35 years in a coal mine, he just lost one finger. My eyes still get misty when I remember the pain he endured as he walked from one room to another with a horrible moan that chilled me to the bone.

The basketball players were the pride and joy of their fathers and mothers, other friends, and neighbors. The high school and elementary schools were dearly loved by the community. When the schools consolidated, it took the heart and the soul of the people with them. It has never been the same.

Since one could not work in a mine if he were not eighteen, basketball was played year-round, usually on a dirt court in front of the elementary schools. It wasn't anything to play six to eight hours at a time during the summer months. This type of dedication led to the outstanding players and teams at the small mountain schools. That didn't mean that the players did not have some work to do. Most people had large gardens; raised cane for molasses; and had small jobs to raise enough money to take in a movie at Reda's Theater in Vicco. The word "farming" has a different connotation for mountain people than for people in central Kentucky. It sometimes became necessary to raise corn for hogs and many other animals on the farm. Also, the corn was necessary to make meal and recycle the meal for corn bread and other products. (I don't care what other people think—if you haven't hoed corn on a rocky hillside with an abundance of copperheads nearby, then you have no conception of hard work.)

In this introduction, I certainly do not dare to leave out

education. Most of our players, beginning with players on the 1928 team, became college graduates. This "yearning for learning" permeated the entire history of Carr Creek High School. There were one or more college graduates from every Carr Creek team from 1928 to 1974! There was never a high school in Kentucky that has had a higher percentage of its students graduating from college than Carr Creek High.

The 1956 Carr Creek team is another example of the truly scholar-athletes. More information will follow as we profile each player and cheerleader. Believe me, they are winners as students in the classroom, as players on the basketball court, and as successful citizens in life.

Educators throughout Kentucky know the high standards of Carr Creek High School. It has always emphasized academics. When I was in high school, if we didn't pass 75 percent of our classes each week, then we sat out of basketball the following week. Starting with the first graduating class in high school (1927), the school has averaged more than 50 percent of its students going on to college—three times over the state average. (At one time, four of the five regulars on the Pikeville College basketball team were Carr Creek products.)

Coach Combs, an unruffled native of Hazard, believes teams win games by their own efforts. But he doesn't discount some "outside aid" his Indians may have had in getting the state championship title.

He talks about how, before a regional tournament game expected to be tough, he walked into the dressing room and found his nine-year-old son, Glen, and the team manager over in a corner. They were devoutly reading the Bible and praying. (It is this type of behavior that has separated Carr Creek from many of the other schools.) It was no accident that Carr Creek's first coach, Oscar Morgan, was a devout Christian. Willard "Sprout" Johnson and Morton Combs, at this writing, are still active members of the church. The Christian influence of these two men cannot be measured. It could be their greatest contribution, much more than wins and losses.

1
Early Season Predictions

Several local and statewide media outlets gave their early season predictions of how Carr Creek would play in the 1955-56 season. Following are a few of these predictions.

"Though the 1955-56 season has hardly begun, there are four teams that stand out from the rest of the 14th Region teams. These four are: Hindman, Carr Creek, Breathitt County, and Hazard. The defending 14th Region, Hazard High, and also winners of the state championship last year, start their season tonight and is expected to be strong again for this year.

"Memorial Combs (4-0) will put their undefeated record on the line against Maytown on Monday and Hindman on Tuesday. Warren Cooper's Panthers, who represented the region at the state tournament in 1954, have scored

314 points for an average of 78.5 per game. Their opponents have 225 and an average of 56.2.

"The Panthers 6-3 center, Charles Kilburn, has scored 73 points, despite a slow start, for an average of 18.2. Carl Reynolds, 6-2-1/2 forward, has scored 67, while 6-1 guard, Johnny Strong, has scored 53.

"Breathitt County (3-1) has scored in the 90's twice, 95–29 over Oakdale and 91–32 over Owsley County. Breathitt averages 84.2 points a game to their opposition's 38.5. They lost their last game 68–64 to Carr Creek at Jackson.

"Hindman and Carr Creek, perennial powers, are also playing in the same district as Breathitt County—the 55th. Morton Combs' Creekers have a 6-1 record. The Indians dropped their first game to Wayland, a 15th Region Team, 70–68, on the Wasps court. Since then, they have defeated Cordia, Powell County, Jackson, Breathitt County, and Garrett for an average of 77.4 a game to their opponents' 62.2." (By C. K. Whitehead, Jr.)

"The Carr Creek Indians have won 16 games in a row, after posting an 81–64 decision over a district neighbor, Breathitt County, on Wednesday night. The outcome was never in doubt as the Indians maintained a wide margin throughout. E. A. Couch dropped in 25 points for the visitors to run his 17-game total to 349. Breathitt County now has a 14-2 record.

"How would you like your hopes of getting out of the 55th district tournament? The state ratings show that five of the top ten of the 14th Region and 13th Region hail from the 55th district comprising Breathitt County and Knott County. Carr Creek is 6th, Breathitt County 10th and Hall High 20th.

"Being in the same district (55th), Hindman, Carr Creek and Breathitt County have the dubious distinction of cutting each other's throat. The Creekers may have a slight advantage over the others. Jackson (4-2) may not have the power to cope with the others, having lost to Carr Creek 92–60. Cordia (5-1) may be a sleeper with only a 72–56 defeat at the hands of Carr Creek, marring their record. Knott County, Oakdale and Riverside completed the remainder of the 14th Region." (Courtesy *Louisville Courier-Journal*)

The following is a rating of the 14th Region by the *Hazard-Herald* prior to the District Tournament in 1956:

"The Carr Creek Indians return to a familiar spot this week. They lead in the weekly *Herald* cage ratings, after a one-week absence.

"The Carr Creekers scorched previously unbeaten Garrett 100–47 Saturday night at Hindman to pick up enough percentage points to move ahead of Hazard. Hindman moved up from third to second place by winning a 71–52 decision over Pikeville. The Hazard Bulldogs slipped to third when it had a close game with the Napier Navajos.

"The powerful Lee County squad advanced another notch this week to move into the fourth slot. Leslie County High slipped to fifth.

"Carr Creek may be a little backward when it comes to communications (there is no telephone in the community), but there's nothing backward at all about the Indians' basketball team. Morton Combs' outfit is up-to-date in every way.

"Eleventh in the Litkenhous Ratings, Carr Creek has won 13 straight games after losing its opener to Kelly Coleman and the Wayland Wasps 70–68 at Wayland. The victories haven't come over any "cream puffs" either. Victims include Berea (5th in the Litratings), Breathitt County (6th) and Hindman (19th). Berea was beaten 59–56, Breathitt County 68–64 and Hindman 79–65 and 66–54. The triumph over Hindman gave the Indians the championship of the Hazard Invitational.

"Proud of their team's success, Carr Creek fans also are inclined to feel proud when desegregation is mentioned. The Indians, you see, have two black boys this season and everything is working out just fine. They are Don Williams and James Higgins. Neither is on the first team but Williams could make the first 10. According to Coach Combs, both are fine, cooperative boys and so far fans have been very receptive."

(This does not surprise me in the least. When I was playing basketball from 1945-48, a lot of my success as a player was from the black players, as we played together on an outdoor court in front of the Breeding's Creek Elementary School at Red Fox. When I lived there, the population was about 50-50 between blacks and whites. We would chooseup sides and it never was an all-white against an all-black team. Most of the players were older than I. We played hard and aggressive—but not dirty. I played with the older guys when I was in the sixth grade. I cannot remember one fight between a black and a white. We are bombarded constantly about our backward mountain people; I guess, in some ways, we were backward, but not racially. We were vanguards in this area. The blacks and whites went to church together. They washed the feet of each other; they worked together, especially in the coal mines—after you work in the coal mines all day everyone was black, and I am proud my dad was a coal miner who loved his job and his family and especially watching his three sons play basketball. Unfortunately, the only thing missing was that blacks and whites did not go to school together. I really never heard it discussed, because it just seemed the thing to do, at that time, in our state. I thought a lot about it. One of my best basketball partners during the summer was black. It bothered me that he had to catch a commercial bus to get to his school in Hazard. It was not free. His family had to pay for this transportation, and I was picked up by a school bus in front of Frazier's store and brought back after school. No, I never told anyone how I felt. Of course, there were some prejudices I'm sure—but I didn't know about it. Yes, I am extremely proud of the 1956 state champs, but I am also very proud that Carr Creek was the first "all-white" school to play an "all-black" school before forced integration.)

"That brilliant 13-1 record has been chalked up despite

the loss of four of last year's first five. E. A. Couch, a 6'1"
senior forward, is the only holdover. Last year's Carr Creek
team beat state champion Hazard twice during the regular
season and lost to Goebel Ritter's Bulldogs in an overtime
period in the 14th Regional Tournament." *(Hazard Herald)*

"A lot of previous state champions—including 1955
King Hazard—have had close calls in district and regional
play. Carr Creek didn't this year, but the Creekers were in
dire danger in three of their state tourney wins.

"In district and regional play, Carr Creek had things
rather easy. Its lowest winning margin was 18 points when
Hindman was conquered, 85–67, in the district finals. Other district wins were over Riverside, 97–49, and Jackson,
73–49. In regional play, the Creekers beat Hindman again,
93–69; defending champion Hazard 56–34 and Whiteburg,
76–46.

"One of the toughest games for Carr Creek during the
season was against Cordia in the Hazard Invitational Tournament during the early season. Carr Creek snatched a
54–52 thriller in a one-overtime game which put 1,086 fans
on edge. Cordia nearly upset the highly favored Indians by
coming behind from a nine-point deficit entering the last
quarter, to hold the Creekers scoreless for nearly six minutes
while forging into a 48–45 lead with 2:25 left in the game. At
this point, Carr Creek coach, Morton Combs, inserted one
of two African-Americans on the squad and although Don
Williams did not carry the Indians to victory, he managed

to rattle the Lions offense and steal the ball once before he was taken out. He was the first player of his race to ever play on the same team with whites in a local gym.

"With his team trailing 48–45, E. A. Couch of Carr Creek narrowed the lead to 48–47 with 1:56 remaining and Bobby Shepherd tied the game with a free toss with 52 seconds left. Another free toss by Shepherd put the Creekers on top with 42 seconds left, but Cordia's Watts came back with a free toss to tie the game with a little over ten seconds remaining.

"Leon Watts again sank one of two free throws in the last few seconds to put Cordia on top 50–49, but he was guilty of fouling Carr Creek's Shepherd three seconds later and Shepherd made one of two tries to send the game to a three-minute overtime.

"A two-handed push shot by Gary Watts sent the Lions out in front 52–50, but Warren G. Amburgey gave the Indians their final lead with a field goal and a charity toss for a 53–50 advantage and Carr Creek froze the ball in the final few seconds and added . . . a point when Couch was fouled with 25 seconds left in the overtime period. Cordia received the ball in the final four seconds but couldn't score. Cordia had lost to Carr Creek 72–56 earlier in the season."

(In 1948, my senior year, we played Cordia in our new gym. We did not take this team seriously. After all, we were ranked in the top five in the state. As the saying goes, they played our socks off for most of the game. I always took great pride in my hustle and defense. His last name was Combs. I was in his face all night and he acted as if I wasn't there. He hit at least 10 shots over me from every spot on the floor. He couldn't miss. We finally won the game—barely. And I always dreaded playing Cordia in the tournament.)

"Cradle of the 1955 state champion, the 14th Region just might be the spawning ground of Hazard's successor. Of course, it's a long way and a perilous road through even the district and regional gauntlets, but Carr Creek has the guns to clear a pass for the state title. First the Creekers of Morton Combs own a handsome 24-3 record against better than average competition. They also have size and an outstanding player in E. A. Couch." (Gordon Moore, *Louisville-Courier Journal,* Feb. 27, 1956)

"The highly-prized Kentucky High School Basketball Championship has rested in the mountain communities of Inez and Hazard for the past two seasons and now two other Eastern Kentucky schools—Wayland and Carr Creek—have aspirations of keeping the title in the ridge country.

"It's a long road for any team that winds up with the big trophy and speculation as to the winner, before the district and regional play-offs get under way Tuesday night is merely wishful thinking. Season play for the 1956 school year is now history and each of the state's 520 basketball playing schools start the long grind Tuesday that could lead to the championship.

"The select sixteen is Kentucky's best from all sections of the state even though many favorites fall by the wayside in the preliminary rounds." (Courtesy *Courier-Journal*)

2
Regional Tournament

The *Hazard Herald* reported on Carr Creek's 14th regional championship win and their progress leading up to the state tournament.

"Carr Creek and Hazard moved into the semifinals of the 14th Regional Tournament, blasting Hindman and Owsley County last night in Memorial Gym in Hazard. Playing before a full house, the Carr Creek Indians knocked off Hindman, 93–69, for the fifth time this season and proved to any doubters in the crowd that it will take something short of a miracle to keep them out of the state tournament.

"Tonight's winners will clash for the regional title tomorrow night at 8:00 p.m. in Memorial Gym.

"Bobby Shepherd and W. G. Amburgey completely dominated the boards for the Carr Creek Indians as the smaller yellow jackets of Pearl Combs who were forced to shoot over a tight defense last night.

"Carr Creek rolled to a 22–10 lead in the first period with Amburgey and Shepherd contributing 10 points apiece. Hindman stepped up the pace in the second period but was still outscored 25–21 and Carr Creek held a 47–21 advantage at halftime. Amburgey dumped in 19 points in the first half, followed by Shepherd with 13. Granville Williams was the leading scorer with 12.

"E. A. Couch came to life in the third stanza and threw in eight points as the Indians breezed to a 79–48 lead going into the final period.

"In the fourth period Carr Creek's second team was put into action, and was outscored by Hindman by only one point, 21–20. Coach Morton Combs' Indians were paced by Amburgey with 24, Shepherd had 20 and Couch 16. The Indians scored 35 times from the field and cashed in on 23–29 free throws.

"Hindman's top scorers were Williams with 23 and James Moore with 19. The jackets could get only 26 field goals, but were terrific at the foul line with 17 out of 21."

(As stated in Chapter 1, Carr Creek breezed through the district games.)

"Only nine personal fouls were charged against them in the regional final, three of those against the second team. After the Indians had picked up a 22-point advantage in the third period, the second teamers got in on the kill.

"Morton Combs, coach of the Carr Creekers, is one of three men who have played on a state championship team and later returned to the Big 16 in the role of coach. Combs was on Hazard's 1932 team. Others who earned gold basketballs and later sought them in a coaching capacity are Paul Jenkins and Warren Cooper. Jenkins played on Manual's championship team in 1923 and coached at Ashland to the state title in 1933. Cooper was a member of the title-winning Brooksville quintet in 1939 and brought Dilce Combs High in 1954."

(In my research about basketball teams and coaches, Morton Combs is the only principal-coach during the same season to win a state championship.)

"The Carr Creek Indians, after a weekend celebrating their status as 14th regional champion, have settled down to the serious business of getting ready for the state tournament. Coach Morton Combs' power-laden aggregation will go into action in the first round of state tournament Thursday at 10:45 a.m. against a strong Central City five in Lexington's Memorial Coliseum.

"The Indians came through as expected to sweep the 14th regional tourney in Memorial gym at Hazard downing Hindman, Hazard and Whitesburg on successive nights. They won with comparative ease, and although the victory in Saturday night's finals over Whitesburg was expected, the team and Carr Creek's fans broke into joyous jubilation when the final horn sounded.

"The Indians proved their power in the tourney at

Memorial gym by overcoming what appeared to be formidable competition in the opening minutes of its game with Hazard and Whitesburg.

"Hazard, whose counterparts of last year won the state tourney, threw a real scare into the Creekers in Friday night's semifinals.

"Coach Goebel Ritter's Bulldogs, who entered the tourney as 54th district runner's up to district champion Leslie County, opened its game with a ball-holding technique. Hazard not only kept possession of the ball most of the first quarter, but led the Indians up until there was less than two minutes of the period. But the Creekers edged out front at the end of the quarter, 18–16.

"Carr Creek came back in the second quarter to also employ stalling tactics, at the same time scoring nine markers against four for Hazard to take a halftime lead of 27–20. The Indians then combined their power on defense as well as offense in the third period, scoring 15 to Hazard's 5. In the fourth quarter, the Indians garnered 14 to Hazard's 9, making the final score 56–34.

"Center Bobby Shepherd paced the Indians with 17 points, followed by Freddie Maggard with 14 and E. A. Couch had 11.

"The Carr Creek Indians (30-3) are no stranger to the state tourney, whether it is held at Louisville or in Lexington's old alumni, or the new Memorial Coliseum. Even the coaching staff remains the same.

"Coach Morton Combs and his assistant, "Sprout"

Johnson, were around when they made that trip in 1928 to Chicago. "Sprout" on the 1928 squad and Morton playing at Hazard. All those years of experience served them well. The squad was sadly depleted by graduation and was counted out in preseason speculation. The Indians' victim Saturday night was Whitesburg 76–46.

"E. A. Couch, the 6-2 forward, was the only returning regular, but along came Bob Shepherd, a 6-3 center from Kingdom Come, and the Indians were on their way again. Combs and Johnson refused to break tradition, and still use a former Carr Creek player, Paul McGranner, as official scorer." (He played on the 1944 team that beat Harlan on their floor. Harlan went on to win the state championship.)

"Carr Creek opened the season by losing to Wayland 70–68 on November 8. They didn't lose again until February by 83–67 at Berea to break a 20-game winning streak. They beat former state champion Hindman, a team that many times have eliminated some of the better clubs in district play, five times this year. Couch rounded out the 27-game regular card with 547 points and Shepherd had 429 at pivot.

"The varsity is made up entirely of seniors, Warren Amburgey; E. A. Couch; Ed Richardson; Fred Maggard and Bobby Shepherd. Jim Calhoun and John Mullins see plenty of action and sometimes start, depending on the team they are to play.

"Carr Creek ended its season by beating Wayland 79–64, despite the fact Kelly Coleman scored 40 points for Wayland. Carr Creek's third loss was to Ashland, the night after losing to Berea. Carr Creek uses a man-to-man defense and at times guards all over the floor. They like the fast-break offense but can score from outside against a zone. Whitesburg was a surprise finalist. They are coached by Ernest Trosper, who graduated from Union College last June.

"Combs doesn't mind a bit meeting Central City's Golden Tide in the big show. He said they'd tackled some of the best in their 33 games and were eager to get on with the job.

"One thing that rides in the Indians' favor is their strong defensive pressure."

3
State Tournament

Johnny Carrico of the *Louisville Courier-Journal* reported: "There will be four newcomers among 16 teams vying for the state tournament this week. The Kentucky High School Tournament, opening Wednesday in Lexington, might as well be styled 'New Faces' of 1956.

"At least four of the sweet sixteen are raw newcomers to the big 'show,' while several others haven't made the state trip since the game 'switched' over from the peach basket.

"The novices are Earlington, Glendale, Boone County, and Bell County. Defending champions who repeated by winning regional finals last night include Mayfield, Henderson, Central City, Shelbyville, and Olive Hill. Wednesday in the Coliseum are Allen County, Valley, Maysville, Lafayette, Monticello, Carr Creek and Wayland. Carr Creek registered one of the widest margins of the night as the high-ranking Indians mauled Whitesburg.

"The Carr Creek Indians, 14th regional champion, will carry the Litkenhous banner in the state tournament at Lexington this week. With Berea out of the running, Carr Creek has taken over the number one spot in the Litratings of state tournament teams. Carr Creek's margin over Central City, the second-place team, is only two-tenths of a point. The Indians mark is 78.5, the Golden Tides 78.3."

CARR CREEK VS. CENTRAL CITY

"In a game that would have been more fitting as a championship struggle than a first-round contest, Carr Creek knocked Central City out of the state tournament with a 70–68 victory in an overtime.

"Freddie Maggard, with the 'Kentucky basketball world' on his shoulders, raced for the goal, stopped 20 feet short and rammed home a one-hander that won the game with a scant seven seconds left.

"Carr Creek came from behind to earn a reprieve on a pair of free throws by E. A. Couch with only eight seconds to go in the regular game.

"They were successful when, with 49 seconds to go, Maggard took over. He drilled cautiously, eying the basket and the Central City defense. With 10 seconds left, Maggard made his move. He came to the top of the circle, aimed and pulled the trigger. Central City had lost in the first round for the third straight time.

"Although Central City went more than five minutes without a field goal, the Tide managed to gain a 14–14 tie at the end of the first quarter. But Central City was in serious trouble when Corky Withrow, the Tide's best player, picked up three fouls in about four minutes.

"Shepherd steered the Creekers through the first quarter, hitting all five of his shots from the field as they ran up an 8–3 lead in just four minutes. With Withrow, Winfred Thompson and Billy Mason cut a 12–7 deficit down to a 14–14 tie.

"With Withrow on the bench at the start of the second quarter, Shepherd and substitute Jim Calhoun pushed the Carr Creek margin to 31–19 with three minutes left before half-time. Here, Coach Delmas Gish wisely returned Withrow to action and he led a nine-point surge that cut the lead to 33–28 at half-time. (Johnny Carrico, *Louisville Courier-Journal*)

"Withrow had a great third quarter as he repeatedly wheeled through the Indian defense, or shot over it. He thumped in ten of the Tide's eleven fielders as Central City dominated the period. When it was over, Central City was in front 55–52 and looked like a winner. Throughout the last half Carr Creek tried to shoot over the Tide defense and was unable to get the ball into Shepherd. Midway in the fourth Carr Creek doggedly fought back and Central City was on top 63–56, but Carr Creek managed to get a second chance and went on to win 70–68." (Special from the *Louisville Courier-Journal*)

Memory of the 1932 finals of the state tournament paid off for Morton Combs, as explained in an article by Billy Surface.

"Daydreaming is usually detrimental to most teams, but a bit of reminiscing on the part of Morton Combs yesterday was particularly responsible for Carr Creek's one-time victory over Central City. After the Indians had just pulled a hat trick to gain a deadlock at the end of the regulation game, Combs suddenly recalled a situation that happened 24 years ago.

"'We (Hazard) were playing in the 1932 state tournament against Louisville Male and the score was tied 13–13,' Combs said. 'And our coach, Pat Payne, ordered us to hold for one shot. I hit the winning basket with only three seconds left and we won, 15–13. I thought we would try to do the same thing in this one time and hoped it would work.'

"The Indian coach could not have used any better strategy. After Central City missed a quick shot, Carr Creek grabbed possession of the ball in the bonus session and held for one attempt. Freddie Maggard swished the net with just eight seconds left and sent the Indians into the quarter-finals against Allen County, a team that Combs has a lot of respect [for].

"'I thought that hitting the basket in 1932 was my biggest thrill,' Combs added, 'but this win today tops them all.'

"Apparently, the Carr Creek outfit, which picked up several backers, including many college coaches, after the squeaker, uses overtimes as its biggest claim to fame. Veteran basketball followers recall the 1928 championship skirmish in which the Creekers and national champion Ashland indulged in the memorable four-overtime affair, and in their last tourney appearance (1948), Maysville required an extra period to oust the Indians in the semifinal. The hero of course was Maggard, who canned the winning basket, but what attracted the attention of college coaches was the steady play of Shepherd and Couch.

"After Carr Creek's thrilling win over Central City, many fans were trying to compare the present squad with the colorful 1928 squad. 'Why, if you got three or four baskets in those days you were a hero,' an observer remarked, while another added, 'they just don't play defense any more'.

"However, Western's Ed Diddle, who witnessed both yesterday's skirmish and also the 1928 encounter, will argue differently. 'They play just as good a defense now as they did in those days,' explained the veteran coach, 'but the thing is though, that the offense has made such a tremendous advance. Why some fellows' favorite shots nowadays never would have been taken 20 or 25 years ago. The offensive type of game is definitely what the fans want,' Diddle added, 'you wouldn't see any game attracting 13,000 even as recently as 1940.'"

The 1928 team

"Their coach was 'drafted' to coach the team because he was the only male faculty member. The eight boys who made the trip just happened to be the best players from the 18 boys in school. There were 23 girls.

"They were given uniforms for use at the tournament by fans in Richmond after Carr Creek won the regional tournament in Richmond. But, they had to borrow U.K.'s blue varsity jerseys for their final when Ashland uniforms proved to be too similar to those bought at Richmond. When they reached the final against Ashland they had set a record that will never be broken. They had won 18 consecutive contests without a substitution, without a time out and without losing a player on fouls. All eight players were related."

(In 1948, Carr Creek won third place in the state tournament, and every starter on the 1928 team was either a cousin or nephew of the starting five on the 1948 team.)

"Morton Combs became coach there in 1938. Even then, the changes were appearing. Dirk had given way. The post office had been changed to Carr Creek. There was no paved road from Hindman, the county seat, but it came soon afterward.

"Take it from the men who know—Carr Creek will be the new schoolboy cage king.

"College coaches are in almost unanimous agreement that Morton Combs' smooth-working Indians are the class of the four-team field that's left in the state tournament shelling.

"Morehead's coach, Bob Laughlin, picked the Creekers to cop the title even before they survived the regional eliminations, and another well-known college mentor explained, 'I just don't see how any of the other teams can match Carr Creek in overall strength'.

"Combs, himself, figures he has seven or eight real good boys and his entire starting combination is a scoring threat.

"'Each boy is a standout in a different way', the successful Indian pilot added. Combs wouldn't elaborate on each player's ability, because he didn't think it would be fair to the team, but a visiting college coach gave his opinion.

"'Shepherd (Bobby) is undoubtedly Carr Creek's top all-around player,' the coach remarked. 'And he's one of the better college prospects in the tournament.'

"Harry Lancaster, University of Kentucky's assistant coach, was highly impressed with the husky pivot man's play and indicated he would talk to him after the tournament was over.

"Dayton and West Virginia also have made an effort to land the 6-3 center. These two schools, also, are after forward E. A. Couch, with Dayton's coach, Tom Blackburn, reportedly having the inside track.

"'Couch is a much better player than his play in the tournament has shown,' Combs commented, 'and he tied Shepherd in the regular season scoring race.' Each posted a 24-point average before the state tournament."

CARR CREEK VS. ALLEN COUNTY

"'Carr Creek—The Overtime Kids,' did it again against Allen County High in the quarter finals of the state by downing Allen County 69–45. Both schools had to go into overtime during the first round to reach the quarter finals. For two quarters, each had put on quite a show.

"Morton Combs' classy Indians, leading only 32–29 at halftime, but clamped down on coach Jimmy Bazzell's fifth region champions in the second half, while improving their own offense. Carr Creek held Allen County to only eight points in each of last two quarters.

"Carr Creek, 14th region king and the tournament favorite by many, had to get a last-second tip-in by big Bobby Shepherd, a smooth 6-4 pivot man, to gain its 32–29 halftime advantage.

"But the Indians murdered the Patriots in the next eight minutes, pulling into a 47–37 lead at the end of the third period. Just about all the Indians were in on the show. Warren Amburgey, Ed Richardson, and Freddie Maggard (whose last-second shot that beat Central City in the opening round). The rugged Shepherd, Couch, and Amburgey gave Carr Creek a hard to beat trio.

"Couch wound up as high scorer for the well-balanced Indians with 18 points, one more than Maggard. Shepherd added 15. Richardson got eight and Amburgey seven."

CARR CREEK VS. WAYLAND Semifinal

The following write-up came from Johnny Carrico of the *Louisville Courier* on March 14, 1956. The headline was "Carr Creek and Wayland Big Threats as State Tournament Opens Tonight":

"A mountain monopoly at Kentucky prep basketball for the past two years threatens to extend its savoy. On the eve of the 39th annual schoolboy's classic which opens here in Lexington tomorrow night in Memorial Coliseum, the mountains' tough combination of Carr Creek and Wayland are given considerable backing. Mountain school's Inez and Hazard won the two previous renewals.

"And it won't be long to find out where Wayland stands. Copper John Campbell's Wasps and their fantastic 'King Kelly' Coleman gets the shenanigans off to a high-class start when they catch Coach Evan Settle's Shelbyville team at 7:30 tomorrow night.

"Carr Creek is the Litkenhous choice in the tournament, with Central City number two, and Wayland number three. The Creekers lost only three decisions over a rugged 33-game schedule. Ironically, Wayland beat Carr Creek 70–68 in the Creekers' first game of the season and Carr Creek beat them 79–75 in Wayland's last game. Many people see these two mountain teams playing in the semifinal.

"The Indians have a pretty fair opening assignment in the tourney, playing a very good Central City team at 10:45

a.m., Thursday. Central City posted a record that matches Carr Creek's season.

"E. A. Couch, a 6'1" forward, Jim Calhoun, 5'11" sophomore guard and Bobby Shepherd, a 6'3" center are the bulwarks of the Indians' offense."

"King" Kelly Coleman

He was sloppy looking and overweight, packing at least 210 pounds on his 6'3" frame, but Coleman became a Kentucky high school legend in 1956. The state champ that year was Carr Creek, but the tournament will always belong to "King" Kelly.

The son of a coal miner, he was raised with ten brothers and sisters on the Right Fork of Beaver Creek in Floyd County. He learned the game on a dirt court, where he would often play until after dark, working on his jumpers and his deceptive moves.

Once he got to high school, he posted a 33.7 career scoring average for the Wayland Wasps of the 15th Region. As a senior in 1955-56, Coleman averaged a whopping 46.8 points; his highest explosion was 75 points against Maytown.

In those days, before the comprehensive media coverage that came to exist later, nobody outside of the mountains of Eastern Kentucky had really seen Coleman until the Sweet Sixteen got under way in UK's Memorial Coliseum in 1956.

His neighbors and fans were so proud of him that on

the opening day of the tournament, an airplane bombarded Lexington with leaflets bearing such messages as "The King is coming" and "King Kelly Coleman Is In Town."

But surprisingly, Coleman got more boos than cheers when he was introduced before Wayland's first-round games against Shelbyville.

One reason may have been that, well, he just didn't look like a basketball player. Coleman has always believed, however, that it was more because he had committed to play his college ball for West Virginia, spurning University of Kentucky's coach, Adolph Rupp. Kelly told a teammate that he did not feel he would have lasted under Rupp. Coleman was the type of player who would later be described as a "free spirit."

Though he was purported to have a high IQ, he didn't care much for academics. In addition, even though he was only 17, he had already acquired a taste for partying. Later, Wayland and Carr Creek, two outstanding mountain teams, met in the state semifinal game. It was a classic matchup, and Carr Creek prevailed 68–67.

The boos before the Shelbyville game hurt the King's feelings so badly that he vowed to show the crowd a thing or two. In the first game he scored 50 points in the game against Shelbyville, and Wayland won 87–76, breaking by 3 Linville Puckett's scoring record for a single game. Said Coleman after the game, "I was only 17 years old and I hadn't been anywhere but up in the mountains. I was sort of surprised at the boos. I did not ask for all the publicity. I have never really liked it because the opposing team used my publicity as a way to motivate the players to play hard against me."

His record performance didn't win the fans over, but Coleman tried to block out the booing and the insults.

After scoring 39 in a 66–58 quarter-final over Earlington, "King" Kelly was "held" to only 28 points Saturday morning in a 68–67 semifinal loss to eventual champion Carr Creek. Said Coleman, "I had a bad case of flu against Carr Creek, which nobody seemed to realize. Everybody expected me to get 50 points every game. If I got 40 it wasn't enough."

In those days, the semifinal losers played a consolation game before the championship. With nothing at stake except his pride, Kelly decided to leave the fans with a little something to remember him by.

He scored 68 points, still the state tournament record, in a 122–89 win over Bell County. His coach, Copper John Campbell, said that Kelly could have scored 100 but Kelly asked his teammates to play it straight and not concentrate on his total points.

Finally, after the 68 points, Kelly left the floor with the crowd's cheering ringing in his ears. But he was so hurt by the earlier booing that he let his sister, Linda, accept his All- Tournament trophy after Carr Creek's 72–68 win over Henderson in the title game. Stated Coleman, "When they handed out the trophies, I was back in the hotel room watching T.V. I felt I had had enough. I thought, to hell with it."

"*Disobeying coach's orders responsible for Carr Creek's narrow semifinal win over Wayland.* Carr Creek's Freddie Maggard, a double-hero during the state tournament, certainly believes in taking things into his own hands. If Maggard, who fired the winning shot against Central City Thursday morning, had obeyed his coach's orders, Carr Creek probably would have been playing in the consolidation game last night instead of the championship skirmish.

"Unlike the first-round battle with Central City, when Coach Morton Combs ordered one of the guards to take the final shot, such was not the case yesterday, although the ending was the same. With the Indians on top, 63–62, Combs called the team's final time-out with 1:41 remaining and instructed them to feed the ball to Bobby Shepherd, if they got behind or the score was deadlocked. 'I knew we couldn't take another time-out so I had to make plans for several different situations like that,' grinned Combs after the victory.

"However, during the excitement, apparently the Indians didn't have much time for thinking. The game was in the dying seconds and Melvin Robinson had just swished in a basket to put Wayland on top 67–66, much to the approval of the capacity crowd. The situation looked dark for the Indians, but Maggard pulled another game out of the fire. 'Of course you can't say anything to the boy (Maggard) after hitting a shot like that,' added the Carr Creek coach.

"Maggard wanted to carry out Combs' orders. 'I sorta glanced up at the clock, and noticed that there was seven seconds left, but I couldn't find Bobby,' exclaimed the hero. 'I thought the time was about all gone so I just fired and hoped it would go in.'

"Maggard's climatic basket was about the same spot as the winning shot against Central City in the opening game for the Creekers.

"Thus for the second in three, Maggard got another 'free ride' from his teammates to the dressing room. A Furman scout, who had been eying E. A. Couch and Shepherd, added the third Creeker (Maggard) to his want list."

Freddie Maggard's winning contribution was also praised in an article by Johnny Carrico of the *Courier-Journal:*

"Freddie Maggard could hang out a shingle in his yard: 'LATE WINNING SHOTS A SPECIALTY.' The dark-haired, slender Carr Creek guard who won the game with Central City in the last seven seconds cut it even finer here this afternoon. He spotted a 30-footer when only three seconds showed on the clock to put the Indians in the finals with an uproarious 68–67 victory over Wayland.

"Mel Robinson had put the Wasps on top 68–66 at 18 seconds with a close-in hit that looked like it might be the ball game. It had been a dogfight from the start with Wayland leading for 18 minutes before Carr Creek passed them.

"Coleman, who had virtually been dormant (for him) the first three quarters, suddenly came to life. He peppered five goals in the last six minutes when it looked like Wayland might put a second loss on the Creeker's books this season.

"Carr Creek kept Coleman pretty well in hand the first

half but the Wasps led 32–28 at halftime, chiefly through the efforts of Elwook Hall.

"The closeness of the game is reflected in the score. In the second half, Carr Creek went ahead for the first time 36–34 a few minutes into the third quarter. There were ties at 32–32, 34–34, 35–35, 36–36, 40–40, and 45–45.

"Carr Creek moved ahead 54–39 early in the fourth, but a six-point outburst by Hall, Coleman, and Robinson gave Wayland a 57–55 advantage. They came down the stretch, head to head, with ties at 57–57, 59–59, and 61–61. The Creekers upped their lead to 64–62 and a tip in by Shepherd that put Carr Creek in the lead 66–62 with 43 seconds left. The teams see-sawed leads down to the final seconds. Wayland scored to put Wayland ahead, but at the horn Maggard hit a 30-footer and Carr Creek wins by one—68–67. Shepherd scored 26 and Couch 17 to lead the Indians."

Earl Ruby had this to say about Carr Creek's surge to the finals in the 1956 tournament:

"Carr Creek's surge to the final round of the basketball state tournament at Lexington yesterday tells a story of progress in the mountains. A story of advancement in roads, electrification, buildings, and book learning as well as athletics.

"Three Carr Creek boys went to Lexington in style. Rated the smartest, strongest team of the 16 contestants, they represent a school of around 490 students 6-12. They have a nice school building and a good gymnasium which seats 700.

"Quite different from those ragged boys who came down

out of the mountains 28 years ago to force a highly favored Ashland team through four overtime periods before losing 13–11 in the championship game.

"Two of Kentucky's leading prep outfits—Wayland and Carr Creek—staged a bitter battle before the largest crowd in Eastern Kentucky cage history Friday night in a gala doubleheader. When the smoke had cleared away, Carr Creek avenged a previous loss to Wayland eased by the Wasps 79–75.

"In the nip-and-tuck fray, Carr Creek's height paid off as 6'4" Bob Shepherd and E. A. Couch out rebounded the smaller and got several easy tip-ins. The Creekers were behind 35–33 at the half as Kelly Coleman scored 26 of the 35 points for the Wasps.

"In the second half, Wayland was leading the Indians six points with seven minutes to go in the half. Then forward Bill Fultz fouled out and Carr Creek came back to tie it at 68–68. With 2:20 left . . . Kelly Coleman went out on fouls. The 14th Region powerhouse, with a 24-3 season record, iced the fray as Maggard and Shepherd hit three in a row; Coleman ended his season's play (he scored 40 points in the final game against Carr Creek) with 1,453 points in 31 games for a nifty 46.9 average."

In the final season ratings for all teams, Carr Creek was the fourth; Wayland was number six; and Breathitt finished number ten.

Johnny Carrico of the *Courier-Journal* reported in

March 1956 the events surrounding the tournament team awarding ceremony:

"You have seen the Litkenhous Ratings of the state tournament field. Now comes the Hooperatings: (1) Carr Creek; (2) Lafayette; (3) Wayland; (4) Central City; (5) Henderson; (6) Mayfield; (7) Valley; (8) Allen County; (9) Maysville; (10) Olive Hill; (11) Boone County; (12) Shelbyville; (13) Monticello; (14) Earlington; (15) Glendale; (16) Bell County.

"The winners of the first round? Your little friend will go with Wayland, Monticello, Olive Hill, Carr Creek, Lafayette, Maysville, Mayfield, and Henderson."

(Mr. Carrico missed two of the first rounds. Allen County beat Olive Hill and Earlington beat Monticello.)

"Some 13,000 fans came to hail the 'King' but it was a 'Queen' who came forward to accept for Kelly Coleman, the first of 10 awards presented last night by Russell Williamson, president of the Kentucky High School Athletic Association, to players chosen for the 39th annual all-state tournament team.

"Call for 'King' Kelly soon subsided when demure 'Queen Linda Carol' Coleman, sister of the illustrious Wayland wonder, took her place at the honor table for the ceremony which included also the presentation of the championship trophy to Carr Creek's Indians for their 72–68 triumph over Henderson's Purple Flash."

"Where was King Kelly? 'He's kinda shy,' explained Linda Carol, and it was evident from her sudden blush that shyness might be a family trait.

"'But where is he?' she was asked. 'Is he still here?'

"The 'Queen' wasn't sure. But she thought Kelly had gone, avoiding the cheers from Memorial Coliseum, where only an hour before he had raced up and down the court to score 68 record-smashing points in Wayland's similarly astounding 122–89 victory over Bell County for third place in the four-day tournament which attracted more than 100,000 fans.

"Finally arrayed at midcourt, along with Miss Coleman, a sophomore at Wayland High School, were the other all-tournament players chosen by votes of coaches, officials, and those along press row: Bryon Pinson, Henderson; Pascal Benson, Henderson; Bobby Shepherd and E. A. Couch, Carr Creek; Harry Todd, Earlington; Corky Withrow, Central City; Dave Eskins, Henderson; Rex Story, Mayfield; and Billy Ray Lickert, Lafayette.

"Some disappointment was expressed by fans over the failure of Freddie Maggard of Carr Creek to make the honor list, and probably justly so. Maggard not only was one of the leaders in the championship victory, but in two earlier contests his winning baskets in the closing seconds of play ensured victory for the Creekers.

"In addition to trophies presented [to] Carr Creek, Henderson, Wayland and Bell County for first, second, third and fourth places in the 16-team classic, there was a trophy for the cheerleading squad from Shelbyville, voted tops among entries sanctioned by the Kentucky Association of Cheerleaders' sponsors.

"Many coaches thought that Coleman gave his best rebounding performance in the semifinal game which Carr Creek won 68–67, considering that there was quite a bit more pressure on him at that time. He had 28 rebounds.

"Several persons have asked where Carr Creek, home of the new State Champs, is located. It hails from Knott County about 10 miles from Hindman, the county seat. Some of the towns near Carr Creek are: Pippa Passes, Fisty, Mallie, Handshoe, Spider, Red Fox [my home "town"], Kite, Omaha, Decoy, Sassafras [where I was born]."

"While shedding tears for Carr Creek's Freddie Maggard, because he didn't make the all-tourney team, don't forget there were some other deserving players. Such as Jack Thompson of Bell County. This tournament was so talent-laden that I believe it's safe to say that outside of about the top five boys, you could pick about 20 other players among them whom there isn't much difference."

(Carr Creek had two on the all-tourney team, Shepherd and Couch; Henderson had three. I would complain about this but in 1928, Carr Creek had four on the all-tourney team and the state winner, Ashland, had just two.)

"The state tournament has proven one thing to me—the days of the two-handed set shots is something of the past. I would venture to say, without having facts and figures to back it up, that at least 90 to 95 percent of the field goals made in the 'Dribble Derby' were one-handed or jump shots. Fans saw on numerous occasions when a player had a clear shot at the basket for a two-handed heave, but he would take a dribble and fire up a one-handed push.

"There is nothing wrong with it, I suppose, if the player hits with regularity, but it seems to me that the days of set shots are gone. About the only players who used the two-handed variety exclusively were John Brock of Bell County and Jim Calhoun." (Courtesy *Lexington Herald*)

CARR CREEK VS. HENDERSON

Billy Thompson covered the final game of Carr Creek versus Henderson: "Carr Creek and Henderson! The Carr Creek Indians, who were denied the Kentucky State High School championship in 1928 in a four-overtime thriller against Ashland's Tomcats, weren't to be denied last night as they toppled the scrappy Hens from Henderson, 72–68, in the title game before a capacity crowd at Memorial Coliseum.

"Carr Creek reached the finals by outlasting Wayland's Wasps, 68–67 on a one-hander in the last four seconds by Freddie Maggard. Henderson trapped Bell County, 78–63, to win a berth in the championship.

"Carr Creek, which was forced to score field goals in the waning seconds of two of its four appearances, wasn't as hard pressed in the championship contest, but there were many anxious moments for the Indians. Freddie Maggard, who dropped in game-winning goals in two tilts, was the big gun for Carr Creek with 18 points, but he received some capable assistance from Bobby Shepherd and E. A. Couch, who tallied 17 points each.

"Carr Creek broke on top after five minutes had ticked off when Maggard sank one of his famed one-handed jumpers to give the Indians a 10–8 lead and from there until the halt was completed, the tribe held the upper hand.

"The Indians held an eight-point lead at the first whistlestop, 23–15, but they upped it up to 10 as the second stanza got under way. The Hens kept pecking away and finally whittled the margin down to four on two occasions, but Carr Creek spurted again and held an eight-point spread, 41–33, as the half-time curtain fell.

"E. A. Couch, who has been 'off' in the state tournament, started out in a better way in the championship tilt by pitching in 13 points in the first half to lead all scorers. Maggard dropped in 10 and Shepherd contributed eight for the Carr Creekers.

"With Maggard, Shepherd, and Couch leading the way, the Carr Creekers out pointed the Hens 19–6 in the third stanza, to hold a 60–49 advantage. The Creekers twice held a 13-point lead, but Henderson sliced the margin in the third period to eleven as the horn sounded.

"A new generation had to mature before it could happen, but Carr Creek finally gained the top prize it missed so narrowly in legendary fashion 28 years ago. The rampaging Indians from Knott County put down a late rally by Henderson to defeat the third region titlists 72–68 in the state championship here Saturday night.

"Followers of Carr Creek felt that the Knott Countians' victory was basketball justice because . . . the 1928 team was defeated by Ashland in four overtime periods.

"The Creekers were a power in Kentucky circles all season and were ranked number one in the tournament by the Litkenhous Ratings. The Indians lost only three games during the season—to Wayland 70–68 in the first game of the season; to Berea 83–67 and to Ashland. They won 25 in season play and 10 more in tournament play from the district through the Big 16 on Saturday night.

"Their progress through the tournament play included victories over Central City (in overtime); Allen County; Wayland; and Henderson.

"1956 was a wonderful year for the Carr Creek team as they won the High School State Tournament by beating three of the strongest quintets in the tournament. The first game against Central went into overtime. Allen County was the only team who just couldn't match the strength and depth of the Creekers, and Carr Creek won 69–45. The third game against Wayland matched the two best teams from the mountains of Eastern Kentucky. The two teams had split during regular season. It was a heart-throbber that kept the entire Memorial Coliseum fans in an uproar. It was a game that centered on the nationally known Kelly Coleman of Wayland. But Carr Creek was much better balanced as a team with every player filling his role. Though Coleman only scored 28 points, a season low, he was a terror on the boards with 28 rebounds. Many observers felt that could have been his best game. Sophomore Jim Calhoun did a magnificent defense on Coleman. Noting in previous games, Carr Creek coach, Morton Combs, noticed that when Coleman jumped in the air to shoot the ball, he leaned forward after his shot. Calhoun stationed himself in front of Kelly, and he was called for two fouls early in the game. This did not help his scoring output. He still was aggressive as his 28 rebounds would indicate. Carr Creek won the game on a last few seconds' shot by Freddie Maggard. The final score was 68–67."

Without a doubt Henderson High was going to be a worthy opponent in the championship game against the Carr Creek Indians. Henderson beat Louisville Valley High by 18 points in its opener. They beat a strong Mayfield team by two points in the quarter finals. Then Henderson beat a surprising strong team in Bell County High. However, it was obvious that their foes were not as strong as the teams Carr Creek faced in making it to the final game. It certainly was another war for the Indians. In the end it was the strong rebounding and size that helped Carr Creek win by four points.

It was the close wins and team determination to win that endeared this team to the mountain people, especially the Hazard fans. It was here that the Carr Creek players and coaches had their first of many celebrations to follow. There was celebration after celebration when Maggard, Couch, Shepherd, Amburgey, Calhoun, and the others returned to the hollows of Knott County, which was still four decades away from its first stoplight. (One finally went up around Christmas 1996, at the intersection of state routes 80 and 160 in Hindman.)

I never felt so proud of our mountain people than when I read that the championship players, coaches, their wives, and the five cheerleaders gave an appreciation banquet for the "Creeker fans" soon after returning to "Carr Creek Hill." The entire elated bank of Creekers shared their conquest in Memorial Coliseum. What a wonderful gesture on their part! This is called mountain "class." Class is doing something good for other people when it is not expected.

Also, Dawahare's clothing store outfitted every Carr Creek player with a new suit. In 1948, my senior year at Carr Creek, our team won third place in the state, after losing to Maysville in an overtime period in the semifinal. I received word (there were no telephones) that Dawahare's in Hazard wanted to see me. They also presented to me a new suit that I wore for four years while playing for Morehead State College.

4

Praise for the Champs

The following information is from the *Hindman News* on March 22, 1956: "The state high school basketball champions, the Carr Creek Indians continue to be the chief topic of conversation in Knott County and the 14th Region after two rousing receptions in Hazard and at Carr Creek High over the weekend. Celebrations for the team began after their victory in Lexington Saturday night.

"Fans from Knott and Perry counties met the team Sunday for a victory parade from Homeplace over Highway 15 to the Perry County courthouse for the official reception and ceremony.

"The police chief of Hazard estimated that the motorcade included about 450 cars that stretched for about one and one half miles. Clad in their blue and white jackets, the

Indians boarded a Hazard fire truck at the mouth of Lotts Creek, with fire chief Lawrence Sizemore as their chauffeur.

"Many persons had waited in chilly weather for more than two hours for the team's arrival from Lexington. In Hazard, a crowd estimated at 1,000 was on hand for the ceremonies on the courthouse steps. Police roped off Main Street in front of the courthouse for spectators. Fans, old and young alike, swarmed around the fire truck when it pulled to a stop. They grasped the hands of the Carr Creek players as well as Coach Morton Combs, and Assistant Coach, Willard Johnson.

"The scene was reminiscent of a celebration held in the spot a year ago when coach Goebel Ritter and his Hazard Bulldogs brought home the state championship trophy.

"The crowd went into a roar as the Carr Creek Cheerleaders gave out with four loud rah's and a chant of 'team, team, team!'

"Robert Mansfield, of Radio WKIC Hazard, stepped to the microphone and said 'Fans, we are sorry to be late, but we stopped at the Owsley County line to put up a sign that says: Welcome to the 14th Region, a permanent home of the state championship!'

"Hazard Mayor, Douglas Combs, greeted the Carr Creek team and presented coaches Combs and Johnson with keys to the city of Hazard. 'I'm mighty proud to present these keys for both of you.'

"Each player then was presented to the crowd—most of

them made brief remarks to the effect that they were truly glad to have won the state title and were glad to keep the state championship in the 14th Region for two times in a row. Here are some remarks:

"Bobby Shepherd, center—'We are glad that we won the championship, and we hope it will be brought back to the 14th Region next year.'

"Jim Calhoun, guard—'We had the best team down there and we deserved to bring it back.'

"Freddie Maggard, forward—'I'm just happy to be on the state championship team.'

"E. A. Couch, forward—'We fought all the way. Although we were in trouble two or three times, we just kept on fighting.'

"W. G. Amburgey, forward—'I think, like the rest of you, that Freddie Maggard deserved to be on the All-Tournament team.'

"Marcus Combs, center—'I'm proud to be a substitute on a team as good as this one.'

"John Mullins, forward—'My teammates have said it all. It was a team effort.'

"Ray Stamper, forward—'I'm just glad to be on this great team.'

"Estill Adams, guard—'We deserved the win. We had the best team and we won.'

"Coach Combs said, 'I'm thankful and proud for many reasons. I just have one criticism, someone stole my hat and coat during the state tournament and it was cold.'

"However, there was a grin on his face, because he would take a state championship win over a coat and hat.

"'I'm happy,' he said, 'for the fine boys we have and for the many good people from this area who were for us.'

"Willard Johnson, assistant coach, stated that we had to win. 'We had too many good rooters back here and we did not want to disappoint you.'

"Willie Dawahare, Hazard merchant and president of the Hazard Booster's Club, said jokingly: 'I might have had something to do with Morton losing his overcoat. There might be another sale at Dawahare's soon. Seriously,' said Dawahare, who accompanied the Indians to the state tournament, 'we had the finesse to perk through the other teams, and we perked when we thought we had to perk.'

"Mansfield, the commissioner of the KHSAA, said he thought the state tourney officials and coaches had made one of their 'biggest mistakes' when they failed to put Maggard on the All-Tournament Team. He said that the Hazard Booster's Club would present to Maggard a statuette like those given to others on the All-Tourney Team.

"Two Carr Creekers, Bob Shepherd and E. A. Couch, were selected to the All-Tournament Team.

"The boys who brought the title here are anything but pampered athletes. Many have a regular schedule of daily chores. Some worked at anything that they could do to supplement the family's income. One particular job, cutting trees underneath electric lines in the heat of the day, made basketball practice a welcome respite from work. There was always time to play outdoors during the summer time. When darkness came, friends and neighbors would position their cars to provide light on into the night. There were a lot of car batteries sold during this time!"

Very few of the athletes were within walking distance of school. They could catch a school bus that eased up the hollows within about a ten-mile radius of the school. Jim Calhoun, a sophomore on the 1956 team, caught a bus at 6:15 a.m. He was from the Yellow Creek area, and it would have been much easier to have gone to Vicco High School in Perry County just a few minutes away. Carr Creek has lost several good basketball players who decided to attend Vicco High.

John C. Mullins, a reserve on the 1956 team, had to leave home at 5:00 a.m. and walk two miles down a path to catch a bus at Amburgey.

It was Carr Creek's fifth trip to the state tournament but the Indians' first title. The most outstanding previous visit was in 1928, when they lost out in four overtimes, 13–11, in the final game to Ashland.

The Carr Creekers also were in the state meet in 1930 and 1931. In 1948, the Creekers finished in third place after losing to Maysville in an overtime game. Don Miller and Bill Morton were chosen on the All-Tourney team.

The following is a story of the 1956 state winners by Joe Creason of the *Louisville Courier-Journal* following the 1956 state tournament:

"Up here, where the scenery is filled with high hills, and

every barn door is decorated with a basketball goal, folks at the moment are living on a large technicolor cloud. For this pinpoint size county community finally has kept a date with destiny after a generation of waiting.

"A week ago, Carr Creek won the 1956 Kentucky High School State Tournament Basketball Championship.

"And the folks who live along Carr, Betty Troublesome, Yellow, Irishman, Breedings and the other creeks that rise far up the mountain hollows of south Knott County couldn't be prouder if the entire area had been selected to be pickled and put on display in the Smithsonian Institute.

"In winning the championship at Lexington, Carr Creek picked up where it left off 28 years ago. Until 1928 when they exploded all over the basketball nation, it was nothing but a remote, unknown mountain settlement school. All basketball fans . . . saw, or read, about this team and the heritage it left for the following Carr Creek basketball teams that would follow throughout the years. This year, the team went all the way, and Carr Creek bounced squarely back into the glory of the headlines."

"Where is Carr Creek?"

When my wife, Sue, and I give the color slide program to civics, churches, and schools, the question most frequently asked of us is "Where is Carr Creek?" Here is what I often want to say:

"Well, it is about five miles from Sassafras and Yellow

Creek; about two miles from Red Fox; about one mile from Cody; about four miles from Dead Mare Branch; Defeated Creek is nearby; about four miles from John D. Smith's swimming hole; and about three miles from the Rainbow Tavern!"

Carr Creek is a creek, a school, and a community all rolled into one. Many of the hollow locations were named after a settler in the coal-rich area. Carr Creek Elementary School and the high school are perched halfway up a steep hillside that rises above the creek on the east side. In 1956, the total enrollment of the high school was around 225 students. About 110 boys were in high school.

The lower grades are housed in two frame buildings that date back to 1920, the year Carr Creek Community Center, which founded the school, came into existence. The high school occupies a two-story native-stone building with an attached concrete-block gymnasium.

Carr Creek is the smallest community in population ever to win the Kentucky High School Basketball Championship. Lying inside are the two road markers that read: *Carr Creek has 20 houses; J. D. Amburgey's grocery houses the post office. The buildings are scattered along the road, Kentucky 160, and up the hill by the school.*

Buses delivered students only as far as the bridge over the creek. Some walked up the rutted winding road to school; others took a steep shortcut path up the hill. Buses used to go to the top. But a few years ago when one was coming down the hill with a load of students, the steering wheel failed on a curve and the bus plunged some 200 feet down the hill. Fortunately, no one was seriously hurt. Many called it a miracle. Since then no buses go up the hill.

When I was in school at Carr Creek from 1945-48, we boys loved to climb the hill to the high school. We always encouraged the girls to go first. Why? The length of the girl's skirts normally covered the ankles, but in walking up the hill the girls had to lean forward, and it was possible to see the backs of their knees. I had mine already picked out and dared the other boys to keep "hands off." But alas, she was just a freshman. It was difficult, but I waited for her sophomore year. I knew it would not be difficult—because I was the basketball "star." We started dating and May 5, 2011, we celebrated our 60th wedding anniversary! I'm positive the "hill" led to many other marriages!

Carr Creek is 12 miles south of Hindman, the county seat, and 22 miles due east of Hazard. It is out of reach of telephones and railroads. When Morton Combs, the principal and coach, came here in 1938, there wasn't even a road over the mountain to Hindman.

The high school building is spotlessly clean and shows the pride of the community, students, faculty, and administration for the school. The inside walls were painted this year, mostly by the students. All the county contributed for the gym that was $5,000. The men and students of the area built it. They later built the immaculate lunchroom and the new home economics room.

5

Post-Tournament Comments

Freddie Maggard was more publicized by not being selected on the All-Tournament team in the 1956 state tourney at Lexington. It seems unusual, but I don't see how the experts left him off. He did a terrific job in the tournament, hitting the winning goals in closing seconds of two of the games and averaging 15.5 point for the four games. The Kentucky Senate passed a bill declaring Freddie Maggard as an honorary all-stater. The House of Representatives did likewise." (Billy Thompson, *Lexington Herald,* March 1956)

"Musings of a dreary-eyed basketball scribe back from the 1956 state tournament. The 39th annual show may go down in history as the best ever, but who knows? Each one seems to get better and it will be bigger when it returns to Louis-

ville for a run at the Fairgrounds Coliseum. Lexingtonians, now that they are almost sure to lose the tournament, are preparing for a fight to keep it.

"Die-hard basketball fans, for whom the season never ends, already are talking about prospects for the next year and are putting the finger on Lafayette, Earlington, Olive Hill and Maysville." (Lafayette won it in 1957.)

"A junior, Jim Calhoun's the best of three Carr Creekers returning.

"When tiny Carr Creek became the 39th state high school basketball champion, the Indians placed Knott County in a unique class. The mountainous county, one of Kentucky's least populous, now can boast of having produced two state champions. Big deal? You say, well yes, it is. Knott County is one of only seven of our 120 counties to produce more than one titlist. Fayette, thanks to five triumphs by Lexington High (now Henry Clay) leads with eight, next comes Jefferson with seven wins. Next are Boyle, Boyd, Perry, Martin, Marshall and Knott (Hindman and Carr Creek)." (Earl Cox, 1956)

"Now that Carr Creek's heart-throbbing victories have guaranteed the mountains another one-year lease on the state prep title, the new cry isn't long live the king, but rather, who's going to end such a reign.

"This mountaineer monopoly won't quite surpass a regime like that of Louisiana Governor Huey Long, but its mode of rule is record-shattering indeed.

"When the Creekers, something of a legendary figure in State Tourney play, out did Henderson, 72–68 Saturday night to take the glittering trophy for the 14th Region for the second straight year, they became the third successive championship outfit from the Eastern Kentucky coal fields. Hazard was the 1955 titlist (the Bulldogs were dumped by Carr Creek in regional tourney play this winter) while Inez won the crown the year before.

"No geographical section has ever held such a tenure, except powerful Lexington Senior High (now Henry Clay) which won the first three state titles (1918-1920). In fact, Carr Creek's triumph equaled a unique 30-year-old mark of two different teams from the same region capturing successive crowns. Besides the Indians and Hazard, only a couple of Louisville schools—Manual and St. Xavier—have been able to manage such a trick, winning in 1925 26 respectively.

"Although Morton Combs' outfit waited until the last split seconds to pull a pair of games out of the fire, its final victory was no fluke. Authority for this is Henderson Coach T. L. Plain, whose team battled the Creekers right down to the wire.

"'They just beat us on the boards,' was the way the affable Plain described the final skirmish. 'I thought we matched them (Carr Creek) pretty well in everything but rebounding, but that was definitely the difference.'

"Statistics, too, will bear this out as the classy Hens outshot their opponents—percentagewise. Henderson fired 61, sinking 27, for a respectable 43.5 per cent. Carr Creek's average was poorer, despite the fact it made two more field goals than the Hens. But strength on the boards allowed the champions more shots. They peppered up 74, winding up with a 39.2 shooting percentage.

"'I don't want to take anything away from Carr Creek,' added Plain, 'but I thought we were at a disadvantage all the way through the tournament. Playing that last game every time certainly showed up on the boys, especially the semifinal game. Fred Schuette was nearly exhausted after the first half of the final game and couldn't even play any more.'

"Naturally, the Indians still were excited when they departed for Carr Creek, where a big reception greeted them upon their return.

"Coach Combs himself said he was certainly worried in the last quarter of the game Saturday night. 'It sorta scared me when the boys started into that early freeze. I'm superstitious over stalling early. I've seen too many games lost that way. The boys played well—they were just great—especially in the clutch. It thrilled me more to win this tournament than it did when we (Hazard) won it when I was playing (1932).'

"A motor-caravan greeted runner-up Henderson at Scottsville yesterday afternoon and escorted the Hens into town." (Billy Surface, *Lexington Herald-Leader*)

6
Coaches

Morton Combs, Head Coach

Coach Morton Combs led a Carr Creek team to a state championship in 1956 and was voted Kentucky's coach of the year in 1963. The outstanding coach, who as a player on the 1932 Hazard team hit the shot to win the state crown, was chosen as one of the 26 charter inductees in the Kentucky High School Athletic Association Hall of Fame.

Coach Combs compiled a winning percentage of more than 75 percent with his 26-year association with the Carr Creek team.

After graduation in 1938 from Kentucky Wesleyan College, Combs came to Carr Creek High as a basketball coach and history teacher. "In 1955," he remembers, "I'm sure we had the best team in the state. We won 31 of 32 games. It was unfortunate that we didn't make it to the state tournament. Hazard beat us in overtime in the regional."

His coaching career was interrupted by another obligation: in 1942 Combs enlisted in the U.S. Army. He served four years, two of those in the European Theatre. After his stay in the army, Combs returned to Carr Creek and continued his coaching and teaching career.

"In all the years I coached, we never played a tournament on our home floor," Combs relates, "It was a big disadvantage. We had two or three teams I truly believe could have won the state tournament—but we didn't have the luck to go along with the skill. Luck is part of it too."

In a conversation with Morton a few years back, he said to win a state championship you have to be good, and you have to be lucky. Two of his teams exemplified this statement about these two ingredients. His 1956 team was good and also lucky by winning games as time was running out. His 1955 team was very good. The 1963 team was plenty good because it won the Louisville L.I.T. over number-one-ranked Louisville Seneca. However, one of his best players, Lewis Couch, was injured and did not get to play in the tournament. Carr Creek High was never the same.

In 1956, Comb's Carr Creek squad did go to the Sweet Sixteen and came home with the trophy. They were given a hero's welcome back in Eastern Kentucky, with a huge crowd meeting them in Hazard.

A particular thrill of his coaching career was being able

to coach his son, Glen, who starred on the 1963 team that was so good. Glen, who went on to star at Virginia Tech and then played professional basketball for seven years in Utah.

"I taught him to play when he was two or three years old," Combs laughed, "indoors with a little ball and a hoop over a doorway." A few years ago Glen was inducted into the Virginia Tech Hall of Fame in recognition of his outstanding play there.

Morton said that he almost left Knott County a couple of times for jobs with better pay, but when it came down to it, he couldn't go. "I thought too much of everyone here. People were too good to me; they spoiled me!"

Combs, a modest, quiet-spoken man, praises his colleagues and credits them for his success.

The man who made it all click: Morton Combs, the gentle scholar. He may have been the quietest and calmest coach ever to win a state title. It was rare for him to raise his voice at his players or officials.

"Instead of raising Cain," Shepherd said, "he got his point across through subtlety. He was a great man."

"He didn't have to yell at us," Couch said, "he already had our attention because he was the school principal. He was a real disciplinarian."

Combs thought he had one of his best teams in 1955, but Carr Creek lost to Hazard in double overtime in the regional. Hazard went on to win the state title.

In 1956, it was the Indians' turn. They had statewide respect and were ranked high among the best in the state. Still,

Carr Creek did little things that, in the words of Calhoun, "gave us a little mountain flair."

"When Carr Creek checked into the Phoenix Hotel for the Sweet Sixteen," Calhoun said, "the first thing we were asked was if we had any uniforms. They were still thinking of the 1928 team," he said.

Combs had been through it all before. In 1932 he hit a shot in the closing seconds to give Hazard a 15-13 victory over Male in the championship game. But he got a bigger thrill out of coaching the 1956 Carr Creek team to the state championship. (In my research, I could not find a coach in Kentucky who played on a championship team—Hazard—and also coached a team to the state championship—Carr Creek.)

"Even when I was in high school I knew I wanted to be a coach," he said. "And it's the dream of every coach to win the state championship. Anybody at a small school has to have some luck along the way to win the state tournament, so I consider myself fortunate."

Morton and his wife, Dale, have lived in the same house for over 50 years right next door to the old Carr Creek High School. In 1974 because of consolidation, Carr Creek High School was closed and along with Hindman High School and Knott County High School, became Knott County Central. Now they have a large modern building with all the modern conveniences, including a swimming pool. The Morton Combs Athletic Complex (named in honor of Morton) at the high school is very modern with a seating capacity of 3,500. The old Carr Creek High School has been remodeled and is now used for Head Start.

Although the Combses spend a few months every winter in Florida, they come home in time for him to attend the state tournament each spring. That's because he is renewed by his memories of that championship season and by the hope that a mountain team can relive the glory of Carr Creek. "I think the mountain teams are coming back."

Coach Combs did not have the best coaching situation in 1938. Even then the changes were appearing—the Post Office Dirk had given way. The Post Office had been changed from Dirk to Carr Creek in honor of the 1928 team. There was still no paved road from Hindman, the county seat, but it did come soon after 1938. Combs helped the people in the community remodel a wooden gymnasium, which had been built with donated money after the widespread publicity of the 1928 team. It had been neglected, after Miss Humes left, and it had large holes in the walls which had to be plastered. The coal stoves were not very effective because of the wind and snow that made it through the cracks in the walls. Morton enjoys telling some of the elementary kids how one little girl in particular was dragging a piece of lumber to the construction site. Just another example of the love and loyalty the community and students had for their school.

One would think that the basketball program at this time could not possibly compete with other area teams. However, that was not the case. The four teams coached by

Morton during the span of 1938-1942 were very competitive. His 1939-40 team lost one game during the season. I can remember some of the players: Vadis Back; Hastel Francis; Ray Combs; Giland Hylton; Gail Amburgey; Ellis Adams; Everett Stamper; George Armstrong; Courtney Combs; Floyd Combs, Jr.; Kermit Combs; Paul Combs; Ernest Sparkman; Dexter Combs; Eugene McLean; Damon Disney; Farmer Couch; and other fine players.

In 1942, Morton joined the army. He was in the Normandy invasion and at St. Lo, which was one of the most bombarded areas in World War II. While taking cover in a foxhole, his buddy remarked that it didn't look like they were going to make it. Trying not to think about their situation, Morton made the remark that he wasn't going to die, because he was going back home and leading Carr Creek High School to a state championship.

I can remember when he returned to Carr Creek in 1946 as the principal. He immediately turned his attention to building a new gym since the old one had burned. Again, the community people, students, teachers, friends, and neighbors did the bulk of the work. At the beginning of the school year 1947-48, we finally finished it before our first ball game. It was one of the proudest days of my life, because I, along with many others, worked all summer on the project. For my first three years we practiced some on our outdoor court until cold weather forced us to go to Vicco to practice indoors. I didn't feel that it was luck in getting to the state tourney. We came close to winning it all in 1948 because the season was not as tiring and we could get to rest more on our terms.

Combs' career was marked with honors. He was chosen coach of the year in the 1962-63 season. The large basketball-shaped trophy he received sits on a bookshelf in his living room. He was elected by regional principals to serve two four-year terms on the High School Athletic Association his last year at Carr Creek.

He coached two East All-Star teams, and one year he coached the Kentucky All-Stars against Indiana, splitting the wins. His record at Carr Creek High School for his 19 years was 456 wins and 148 losses without a losing season.

Combs gives high praise to his assistant, Willard "Sprout" Johnson. Johnson was a successful head coach at Carr Creek for 13 years. There was not another team in the state that could match this coaching combination in basketball coaching experience.

In 1970, Combs became the superintendent of Knott County schools, a position he held for eight years. Now retired, Morton and his wife, Dale (Smith), enjoy their home overlooking Carr Creek Lake. Next door is the old W.P.A., native limestone high school building, where he coached for many years. His friend, "Sprout," lives nearby on Carr Creek Hill.

When their daughter Susan was born December 24, 1951, Morton said that was Dale's Christmas present to him! Susan graduated from Carr Creek in 1965 where she was a four-year varsity cheerleader from 1966 to 1969 for her father's Carr Creek Indians. She graduated from the University of Kentucky with a major in Spanish. In 1975, she graduated from the University of Tennessee with a masters in Spanish, and she teaches at Duluth High School in Duluth, Georgia. She married Mr. James (Jim) Hammack. They have two sons, Ryan and Tyler.

Morton and Dale had another son, Len Morton, a fraternal twin of Glen. They were born October 30, 1946. Naturally, they were the joy of Morton and Dale's life. They were loved and spoiled by every Creeker. Then on July 11, 1950, beautiful little dark-haired, dark-eyed Len Morton "became an angel." The following year, 1951, beautiful dark-haired, dark-eyed Susan was born, bringing joy to the entire Carr Creek Hill, as well as to Morton, Dale, and Glen Combs. (Courtesy of Sue W. Miller)

Few people know the humanitarian side of Morton Combs. Like most mountain men, he is hesitant to give personal information that some people might consider bragging. If there was an outstanding student or someone who had the potential to be outstanding, Morton personally would see that this student would have the financial backing to enter college. (I am not going to mention names, but I do know that he helped one of my student teachers, and she graduated from a well-known university and earned her master's degree, and then earned a doctorate in nursing. She is presently teaching at a major university in the northeast region of the United States.)

Now, not all the students did this well, but she proved that you can succeed even if you did graduate from a small high school.

I started my teaching and coaching career at Trimble County High School. It was a rural-oriented county, and we had some very poor kids. I always felt uncomfortable when the principal showed a movie on Friday, and those who could not afford twenty-five cents had to go to study hall.

My wife, Sue, said that didn't happen at Carr Creek. Morton would see that these students were not left out, and he would do it in a way that was not embarrassing to the students.

"The largest 'cottage' built by the early Carr Creek Community Center—today, a three-story chocolate brown with snow white trim—is the home of Morton and Dale Combs. It is next door to the old limestone high school building and cinder-block, half-domed gymnasium. It has a beautiful white fence around the property, reminding us of the bluegrass specialty. The Combs' home overlooks the Carr Creek Lake. The large flat area—and flat areas on the Carr Creek Hill are scarce—is just beyond the white fence and in front of the old school. Every graduate of Carr Creek High School has a strong feeling for this flat piece of real estate—it literally could have been called the Indian Gathering Ground. It was the only place to gather before school, during lunch recess, and after school. The famous outdoor basketball court of the 1928 Class 'B' Champions has been incorporated into the Indian Gathering Ground. The whole scenario is 'hallowed ground' to every 'Creeker.' However, it is home to Glen and Susan (Hammack) Combs." (Sue W. Miller)

Willard "Sprout" Johnson, Assistant Coach

Have you ever heard anybody say any derogatory remark about "Sprout" Johnson? Everyone whom he has taught or coached at Carr Creek High has nothing but praise for him, because he loved his students and players—and we all knew that to be true.

He had a very humble personality and he put his players and students first (not counting his family). He liked to win but always did it fairly and he would never run-up the score on the opposing team. I remember in one game that we were up 20 points after the first quarter, and he sent me to the dressing room, and I came back dressed in my regular clothes and the game was over for me. At the half he had Bill Morton and Paul Gene Francis to get dressed. Sprout was doing two things. One, he was trying to keep down the score and two, he was saving us for a tough game with Louisville Male the next night. (After being behind 17 points in the third quarter and we roared past them and we won by two on a last second shot by Wiley B. Stamper—his only basket! "B" claims that he was the best shooter on the team—we seniors would not pass him the ball.) It has been over 60 years since we won that game, but it sticks out as one of the finest games we ever played.

I have often heard that Sprout was too good. I personally do not subscribe to this theory. I don't feel that anyone is "too good."

Sprout was head coach at Carr Creek for 13 years and had a winning record of more than 70 percent of his games. The gymnasium was completed my senior year (1948) and we almost won the state tournament (finished third).

Maysville beat us in an overtime period in the semifinal. We did not get many breaks from the officials in the last 30 seconds, but Sprout never mentioned that and he took the loss like a man.

When Sprout retired in 1972, former students and players of Carr Creek High School returned to give him a stunning reception at the gym. It was a surprise and it left him speechless. The event was organized by Ernest Sparkman, president and owner of a radio station in Hazard. Several players, including myself, got up to the mike to say a few words in Sprout's behalf.

Sprout told the audience that if he had to do it all over again, "I would be right here at Carr Creek teaching and coaching. I loved every minute of it."

In 1991, Sprout was inducted into the Knott County Hall of Fame. Sprout was on the famous 1928 squad. Carr Creek has gone to the state tournament five times: 1928, 1930, 1931, 1948, and 1956. He has had a part in all the five state teams, either as a player or as a coach.

Though he was better known as a coach, he had found peace in serving his Lord for years as a Sunday school teacher and as other positions at Smithboro Baptist Church, Sassafras, Kentucky. He was not afraid of death.

He was born to Simeon and Alice Francis Johnson at Cody. He attended Carr Creek Elementary and Carr Creek High School. He went to Morehead State Teacher's College on a basketball scholarship. He was the grandson of Fielding Johnson, one of the founding fathers of Knott County.

One of his best decisions was when he married Nelle Hays, the daughter of Senator Doug Hays of Maytown. She also taught at Carr Creek all these years. They had a great marriage and don't just love each other—they also respect each other. Nelle is a strong Christian and lives it every day. I could write a book about her. Sprout and Nelle had two children, Richard Douglas (Rick) and Ann Kathleen. Richard and Glen Combs were the mascots for the 1956 team. Glen was the only Carr Creeker to play professional basketball for several years. He now lives in Roanoke, Virginia.

Now comes the hard part. On Tuesday afternoon, February 15, 2000, Sprout passed away from complications due to strokes. He was buried at noon, on February 18, 2000. He would have been 90 that May.

Sprout and his wife have been my second parents. He was a devoted Christian man and loved the Smithboro Baptist Church at Sassafras. It is the loss that hurts. But we have our wonderful memories.

Ann Kathleen Johnson Pratt

Ann Kathleen Johnson, a "Carr Creek Hill Blue Blood," was brought home from the Hazard Hospital to the "early

Community Center Cabin," by parents, Willard "Sprout" and Nelle (Hays) Johnson. (She is now making that cabin home again, sharing it with husband, Denver, and mother, Nelle, since Mr. Johnson passed away.)

Ann attended Carr Creek Elementary School and Carr Creek High School, gleaning every morsel of solid academic education possible from the gifted faculty. She graduated in May 1958 and enrolled at Georgetown College, Georgetown, Kentucky, as a Business Education major, obtaining her Bachelor of Arts in 1962. In 1961, Ann became Mrs. Denver Pratt—a young man from Lexington, Kentucky, who looked like the antidote to full-time studying to Ann. However, when Georgetown classes began that fall, Ann Kathleen, with a new last name, took a seat for her senior year. This serious student from the "Carr Creek Hill" graduated in the spring of 1962. She uses her business degree part time and, other than being a strong family-oriented person with two daughters, she most enjoys teaching the students at Hazard High School, where she has been a substitute teacher for years.

7
Carr Creek 1956 Champions

Warren G. Amburgey,
1956 Carr Creek Basketball Champion Forward

Warren G. Amburgey had the benefit of an "in-home coach" as a young boy. Older brother Jesse Lee worked hard teaching fundamentals and guard moves to small Warren G. Jesse Lee played guard for Carr Creek High School from 1948 to 1952, graduating in May 1952.

Warren G. relates how ill he became with rheumatic fever in the eighth grade. He was the smallest boy in the Carr Creek Elementary School's eighth-grade class. So, his "in-home coaching" was all important to a sick little boy. Therefore, he was two years late beginning his basketball playing

(1952) and two years late in graduating from high school. He graduated in May 1956.

That year, 1956, was a banner year for Warren G. Amburgey. In January, he and his young wife (Betty Sue Amburgey), having married during his sophomore year, became parents of Donald Wayne (namesake: Freddie "Wayne" Maggard and Donald Hylton, manager for the 1956 team—best friends, classmates, and basketball teammates). Nearly "a lifetime" before the March basketball tournament began. Freddie tells the story of the day in January when Principal Morton Combs came over the school public address system with a curt message: "Warren G. you are needed at home immediately!" He knew he was being summoned to take Betty Sue to the Hazard Hospital for delivery of the expected baby. Freddie being the only basketball team member with a car—the "old gray Plymouth," and having it parked on the Old Indian Gathering Ground in front of the school, jumped out of his seat and the two teammates drove "too fast" to pick up the young mother-to-be. They arrived at the hospital just before Donald Wayne Amburgey. A new Creeker was born.

The new mother and baby (Donnie) settled into a routine of nurturing and keeping "Poppa's" home life comfortable so he could continue his studies and practicing and playing basketball for the road to the state championship.

Warren G.'s road to the state championship began in the fall of 1955 during preseason practice according to Coach Combs. "He 'roughed up' his teammates under the goal so much that I knew I would start him," Freddie Maggard says. He tells how "few could move him out of his position once Warren G. was in his territory—it belonged to him." Freddie says that "he could leap so high above the rim of the basket that one could hear his fingernails scraping the steel rim."

In discussing the 1956 champions Coach Combs stated "Warren G. was a good basketball player." Strong, smart around the goal, and hard-working seems to be the consensus of the coaches and teammates. He was a true Creeker in spirit, a good husband, and a loving father.

Warren G. Amburgey, the youngest son of Arnold and Dessie (Dessie was an early Carr Creek Community Center advocate: teaching, nursing helper for nurse Upton, tidying up the library—anything she could do to make the school succeed in becoming a strong academic environment), was raised on Wolf Pen Creek above the Carr Creek Lake. He was a strong, hardworking family man, in control of his life with beautiful Betty Sue Amburgey and two healthy, beautiful children, Donald Wayne and Margueta Lynn.

Then, in 1992, absolute devastation struck in the form of an automobile accident, killing Betty Sue and leaving beautiful Margueta with ten percent chance of living. After he lost his Betty Sue he turned to protecting his children. Margueta lived and there is no way of saying how much the strong sense of family played in to her recovery. She was cared for by Grandma Dessie, Granddad Arnold, Uncle Jesse, and Aunt Betty and received continuous love and encouragement from Warren G. and brother Donnie.

Margueta was not to know total recovery. She was left legally blind and has some other impairment. She attended the Louisville School for the Blind for nine weeks after the partial recovery of the accident to help her learn to be self-sufficient. Dear reader, if you ever experience depression for a single day you should know Margueta Amburgey (Patton). She is the most optimistic woman you will find. She cares for herself and her home, and can go next door to brother Donnie's home and business alone. She does not drive an automobile but has few limitations. This beautiful former Carr Creek High School cheerleader (1972, '73, and '74) and graduate of Knott Central High School's first graduating class in 1995 "is sunshine on a rainy day."

Warren G. Amburgey has found another beautiful mountain girl to love, to marry, and to be a friend to his Margueta Lynn and Donald Wayne, Jolene Combs. She and son, Dustin Combs, have become a loving and valuable part of Warren G.'s family.

E. A. Couch,
1956 Carr Creek Basketball Champion Forward

The University of Kentucky gave basketball scholarships to Couch and Bobby Shepherd. Before E. A. went off to the University of Kentucky, he married the captain of the Carr Creek cheerleaders, Janie Calhoun (Jim Calhoun's sister).

"I ended up with a family, and that was great, but getting

married shot my career at Kentucky," reflected Couch, some forty years later from his home south of Paintsville, where he moved when his children were young. "Coach Rupp didn't like married players. He had some over the years, but he didn't like it. The situation was bad for me as a player— being away from my high school teammates, and not getting enough food to eat. UK gave me books and a thousand dollars a year to live on. That was it.

"It was hard all the way around. The experiences of the Eastern Kentucky player in general was that Rupp didn't like them. Everybody always thought he did, and he did recruit a lot of them, but when we got there he talked about our area in a derogatory manner. It destroyed the confidence of many of the players from Eastern Kentucky. Johnny Cox overcame it. Don't get me wrong, Rupp was a great coach, but only for a certain type of player. Some of the players who weren't close to their high school coaches got along okay, but I was used to having a good relationship with my coach. Our coach and assistant coach lived right next to the school, and I lived ten miles away, so the coaches were always there and took care of us. At Carr Creek, I knew my coaches really cared for me."

Like most other schools in Eastern Kentucky, family connotations seemed to carry with the players. It started with his father, one of nine Couch brothers who made up the Blue Bird Coal Company basketball team. The elder Couch was offered a contract with the Cincinnati Reds, but the coal mine paid more—especially for a minor league baseball player. Perpetuating the Couch tradition of sports and family, E. A. Couch would send a couple of his own sons to college on athletic scholarships. Joey (John Pelphrey's Paintsville teammate) went to Kentucky for football (he had enough basketball talent to play in several Division I schools), and Joey played at the defensive nose guard position at U.K. He won the respect of his coaches, teammates, and fans because of his great personality.

There are several well-documented reasons Shepherd left U.K. after one year and E. A. after two years, but probably the most important reason was that the Appalachian boys felt alienated in Lexington. This is understandable. To them, a mountain was a place where nobody was around but family; a large campus was a place where everybody was around but family.

E. A. had another basketball thrill of a lifetime—he and his teammates won the National Invitational Tournament (N.I.T.). The marriage to Jane Calhoun was much more acceptable to the coach; thus, at least two major obstacles had been hurdled. The living was easier, the classes were enjoyable, and the basketball arena was a comfort zone. E. A. Couch had made a good move in transferring from his beloved University of Kentucky to the University of Dayton. Meanwhile, wife Jane continued her 4.0 education as well.

E. A. Couch graduated from the University of Dayton and immediately began using his business administration degree at the Ford Motor Company Plant in the Oil Filtering Division. He did well and became a production supervisor.

He and Jane were the parents of two young boys, David and Joey. After Jane graduated from the University of Dayton and obtained her Master of Arts, they made a decision to return to a small town in Kentucky to raise their young sons. They felt a small town would offer the atmosphere conducive to educational development and a safe athlete-type environment, and they chose Paintsville.

It has been said that without All-State E. A. Couch, Carr Creek would not have been the champion in 1956. His very name was synonymous with tenacity and one-hundred-percent effort each time he took the floor in the blue-and-white Carr Creek uniform. He was a quiet, easy-to-smile type of young man, an all-South honoree after he helped Carr Creek win the Kentucky State High School Basketball Championship. He was a hardworking student in the classroom and graduated in May 1956.

In the fall of 1956, E. A. enrolled in school at the University of Kentucky on a basketball scholarship. He had confidence that he was academically as well as athletically prepared to meet the University's standards. However, E. A. did not foresee the "gut-wrenching" problems he would be expected to solve as a freshman college student trying to measure up to the old taskmaster—Adolph Rupp—in basketball, trying to adjust to the large student population and find his way around the U.K. campus and the city of Lexington. These were difficult problems for the shy, good-natured, bright basketball star that was also in love. As stated elsewhere, he and longtime high school sweetheart and chief cheerleader, Jane Calhoun, were married. That gave him a highly intelligent-sounding board at home, but compounded his problems with Coach Rupp.

After E. A. Couch's super basketball season in 1956, he was heavily recruited by the University of Dayton, Dayton, Ohio. However, he accepted the basketball scholarship that Coach Rupp offered, and had E. A. owned a crystal ball to help him see into the bleak future one year later, he surely would have taken a longer look at the University of Dayton. E. A. and Jane realized that emotionally, the young superstar needed to make the decision to call the coach of the University of Dayton to see if his scholarship might be available.

The acceptance of the full basketball scholarship to the University of Dayton was a positive move for young E. A. He excelled on the basketball court as well as in the classroom, majoring in Business Administration while playing basketball for the University of Dayton.

In Paintsville, Kentucky, E. A. obtained a job as a supervisor in the nearby oil fields. He continues to work, to enjoy the careers of Jane, David, and Joey, and reflects on another positive decision in bringing the two young sons to Paintsville to become stars in the classroom, on the basketball court, and on the football field. Both sons have shown the tenacity and academic perseverance in college and in their careers.

It is poetic justice for E. A. Couch, star forward, for Carr Creek High School 1956 Champions to have his youngest son Joey become a champion nose guard for the University of Kentucky playing and rooming with Freddie Maggard II, son of E. A.'s friend and teammate Freddie Maggard, Carr Creek's star guard. While E. A. left Coach Rupp and the University after two years, his son played and roomed with Freddie Maggard II for five years and also scored in the classroom.

E. A. Couch sent his math-oriented son, David, who played basketball for Paintsville, to West Point after graduation. David received an appointment to the United States Military Academy, West Point, in New York. David was given a full basketball scholarship to play for Coach Krzyzewski (Coach K). He graduated, majoring in math and computers, and is the Commissioner of Technology for the state of Kentucky. He is a devoted husband and father and a loyal "army man"—a West Pointer.

Jim Calhoun,
1956 Carr Creek Basketball Champion

Jim is the son of Harold and Delora Calhoun. Like many of us who played basketball for Carr Creek, Jim is the son of a coal miner, a foreman of a mining crew at Blue Bird Mining Company at Anco, Kentucky. The mining company was one of three mining companies that was located on Yellow Creek, Sassafras, Kentucky. (Not far from the Blue Bird Mining Company was the Wisconsin Mining Company where my father, Luther Miller, worked.) The type of mining that existed at this time (early 1940s and 50s) was called deep mining, in which the mining crew would go deep inside the mountains and follow the seam of coal. The miners used dynamite instead of the modern technology used today. The coal was shoveled into the coal cars by their individual workers. It was extremely dangerous work. The seam could go up to three or five miles under the ground. But the miners loved their jobs and took great pride in their work.

Most of the miners on Yellow Creek loved to support their local elementary and high school basketball teams. Jim started playing elementary basketball at the Yellow Creek Elementary School. His coach and principal, Vesper Singleton, played on the 1948 basketball team at Carr Creek that won third place in the state that year. Several players at Yellow Creek Elementary were very successful high school players at Carr Creek High.

Jim's father, Harold Calhoun, had his company build a full regulation-size basketball dirt court out of a mountain with a bulldozer next to the Calhoun's house. It gave the young players a place to learn basketball in a wholesome environment. The better players went on to play at Carr Creek High School.

Other communities with good basketball teams at the elementary level that sent good players to Carr Creek were Breeding's Creek Elementary, Irishman Creek, Smithboro, and Carr Creek Elementary. Most of the other small communities sent their students to Hindman.

Jim was just a sophomore among the 1956 state champions (the others were mostly seniors), but he played a key role in the success of the team during the season and in the tournaments. He played a major role in Carr Creek's one-point victory over Wayland High School in the semifinals of the state. Carr Creek played Wayland in its first game of the season and lost in a close game, and in its season-ending game Carr Creek won in a close game. Jim was assigned to guard "King" Kelly Coleman in their last game of the season and did a fine job of guarding him in Carr Creek's win.

Carr Creek saw a flaw in Coleman's jump shot. When he jumped up for a shot, he had a tendency to lean forward. So acting on this flaw, in the first quarter, Combs had Jim plant his feet and not move. Twice in the first half Jim drew two quick fouls on Coleman as Coleman leaned into Jim on his follow-through—the fouls were called on Coleman for charging. This played a big role in Carr Creek's winning the semifinal game of the 1956 state tournament.

The following may not be all-inclusive, but Jim Calhoun did a good job in remembering the players who went on to play for Carr Creek High:

"I have a nephew David, Joey's brother, and these nephews are the sons of E. A. Couch (1956 Carr Creek Champ) and Janie, a cheerleader of the 1956 squad. David is a West Point graduate and a top basketball recruit for the Army team (Coach Mike Krzyzewski recruited David). My sister, Sue, has two wonderful daughters, Tammy and Robin. It is a very productive family and they are, you might say, carrying on the tradition of the family.

"I was the first of our clan to graduate from college (the

University of Cincinnati, with a full basketball scholarship).
My sister attended Berea College, and E. A. went to the University of Kentucky on a basketball scholarship."

After two years at Kentucky, he graduated from Dayton and played basketball there.

Sue and I shall never forget the first time we met Jim—in Lexington at his "door business." He was talking to some customers, so while we waited we looked at one wall that had all kinds of pictures of Carr Creek and the University of Cincinnati. We felt at home immediately. Sue and I did not know the players on the 1956 team, because I was coaching at this time. We have met all except one—Bobby Shepherd (but we have talked to him twice on the phone).

One of Jim's favorite pictures has him, E. A., and Freddie walking down the road close to Blue Bird Coal Camp, just after they won the state championship. Each has on a Carr Creek jacket. It was so cold so they have their hands in their pockets. They are spaced about four feet apart, which I'm sure came from Coach Combs, when he yelled "balance the floor!" E. A. and Jim had on khaki pants, and Freddie was dressed in blue jeans (same thing we wore in 1948). In the background loom the high mountains that all of us find so familiar. A few houses are also in the background.

But the most telling thing for me in these photos was their expressions, which said to me, "Yes, we won the state basketball championship, but we have not changed that much. Yes, we are extremely proud of our accomplishment, which no Carr Creek team duplicated, but we shall never be ashamed of our heritage. We are just real good friends, and we shall remain that way for the rest of our lives."

Jim gave a lot of the team's success to the leaders (coaches) and to his teammates. No one *gives* you a state championship, but by playing hard, keeping in good physical shape, and playing with a team concept, good things can happen. The 1956 team is proof of that.

Below are words from Jim that demonstrate his gratefulness and attribute his success to those around him.

"As a student at the University of Cincinnati, I had to take seven classes. There were students in my classes from New York, Chicago, foreign students, Louisville, Dayton. I'm sitting there thinking that most of these students come from urban areas and here I am from a very small school, and I am thinking, Am I strong enough to compete with these students academically? Then, after the first semester, I saw many students in my classes packing their bags and leaving for home. The real reason was they were flunking out. I would like to say to my teachers at Carr Creek—you were incredible, you taught us well, you cared for us, and I would like to say thank you from the bottom of my heart. I had to leave before I realized your role and preparation that allowed me to succeed.

"I played all over this country in places like the Madison Square Garden in New York, Chicago, Cleveland, Kansas, Missouri, and many others, and I give a lot of credit to Carr Creek—to keep trying . . . work hard, and do the right things.

"In my sophomore year we had a 28-2 record. I had the

opportunity to play with Oscar Robinson, one of the greatest who ever played the game.

"In my junior year we played in the Philippines and Honolulu and several other places, which is an education itself. I spent five days in Hong Kong and Tokyo, Japan. These wonderful experiences [are] because of basketball. Basketball gave me a chance to excel and it all began at Anco, Kentucky. Thank you, Dad, for building that outdoor basketball court for us. Then to win back-to-back national champions, it was just incredible."

Jim sincerely mentions his experiences at Carr Creek that allowed him to go out in the world and succeed. Jim has supplied me with material after material (pictures) that has helped tremendously in my writing this book. After all these years his enthusiasm has never waned. He is a true mountain person and a great friend to his heritage.

A story from Jim: "Years ago, when the Cliff Hagan's Restaurant opened up, I was in the restaurant on Winchester road, when in walked Cliff Hagan and this big burly guy, who had on coveralls and a long beard. The big guy came up to my table and said, 'Hey, Calhoun, you don't remember me, do you?' In all honesty, I could not recall his name. He said to me, 'Let me refresh your memory. Carr Creek came to Berea in 1956, and we beat you state champs seven points, do you remember that?' Cliff Hagan was looking at me to see how I was going to respond. I finally said, 'No, I don't remember that, but I know when Berea came to Hindman and we beat your butts by eleven points.'

The man was Darryl McNeal, who played with Don Mills. Both went to the University of Kentucky. Berea had some real good teams when Bill Harrell coached there.

Jim talks about the close games that they won in the 1956 state tournament. In the first game against Central, Carr Creek won in an overtime game. Central City was in the western part of Kentucky and Carr Creek in the eastern part of the state, so each team knew very little about the other. It turned out to be one of the best games in the tournament. The same can be said when Allen County played Carr Creek in the quarter finals. Neither knew very much about each other. Carr Creek easily won that game by 24 points. That was their last easy game.

The only team that Carr Creek knew was Wayland. (Everyone knew about "King" Kelly Coleman. They had split in two seasonal games.) It was a classic. Carr Creek finally won by one on a last-second shot by Freddie Maggard. Jim did a great job on Coleman and limited him to 28 points. Coleman was sensational in the rebounding department, hauling down 28.

In the final game, Carr Creek knew something about Henderson, another western Kentucky school. Carr Creek won by four in a very tough game.

Here is another story told by Jim: "I was at a yogurt stand here in Lexington about three years ago. I was standing there eating and I had my Carr Creek jacket on. On the back was *Carr Creek, 1956 State Champions.* An elderly gentleman came by and said, 'You know that Carr Creek thing is just a myth. There was no such place. I have heard of Carr Creek all my life, but no one knows where it is.' At first I figured he had something against Carr Creek—maybe Carr Creek had beat his team, and I wasn't sure what to say. There was a little old lady behind the counter, and as I turned to say something back to him, she said, 'Listen Mister, there is a Carr Creek. They always had good basketball teams and their players were always great, and I will tell you why. I was a cheerleader and I'm from Fleming-Neon, which is very close to Carr Creek.'"

I'm sure that Jim had no idea that his help was going to be a little old lady from Letcher County. The man departed and he did not say anything else. (I was doing some comparison with Jim's teams and our 1945-48 Carr Creek team. Jim's 1956 team beat Hindman five straight times. My 1948 team that went to the semifinals never came close to that. As I recall, my four years on the varsity, we split our games with Hindman and Vicco, our two biggest rivals. Hindman and Vicco had very good teams when I was playing. Like the 1956 team, we never had the opportunity to play one single tournament game on our floor. My senior year in 1948, we finally got our new gym completed and we almost won the state. People at Hazard have always supported Carr Creek—so I don't want to upset the nice people of Hazard—but in my four years at Carr Creek, we never lost to Hazard and we won all games against Breathitt County.)

Jim also states that the 1956 team never lost a game in the 14th Region. That is called domination!

Another interesting story by Jim: "The guys from Yellow Creek formed a team (high school age) and they called themselves the Yellow Creek Globe Trotters. On this team were Cotton Hanks (married my first cousin, Pat Miller), E. A., Jim, Bobby Sorrell, Ford Cornette, Jimmy Everage, 'Super Duck' Miller, and Lowell Thomas, and they went to a basketball tournament in Knoxville, and we won the tournament. It was an independent tournament and teams from other states were involved."

Freddie Wayne Maggard, 1956 Carr Creek Basketball Champion Guard

The following was written by Mike Fields of the *Lexington Herald-Leader* concerning the 1956 Carr Creek team.

"*March 15, 1956.* Freddie Maggard fires in a 22-foot jump shot with eight seconds to go in overtime to give Carr Creek a 70–68 victory over Central City in the first round of the Sweet Sixteen at U.K.'s Memorial Coliseum. Maggard hits a shot from almost the same spot, just above the top of the key, with four seconds left in a 68–67 semifinal win over Wayland and King Kelly Coleman two days later. Carr Creek goes on to win the state championship, beating Henderson City in the finals.

"*March 15, 1987.* Freddie Maggard who now lives in Cumberland, has come back to Carr Creek on a quiet Sunday afternoon to visit with his former coach, Morton Combs, and a couple of teammates, Jim Calhoun and John

C. Mullins. After watching a NCAA tournament game on television at Combs' house, the four men walked next door to the Carr Creek gym. It is dark, dusty and desolate. Maggard finds a basketball in a corner, steps onto the court and fires up an awkward 22-footer from the key. It misses. 'It has been a long time,' Maggard says with a laugh."

Below read presentations for Freddie Maggard:

THE AMERICAN'S CREED by William Tyler Page

I believe in the United States of America as a government of the people, by the people, for the people; whose just powers are derived from the consent of the governed; a democracy in a Republic, a sovereign Nation of many sovereign States; a perfect Union, one and inseparable; established upon those principles of freedom, equality, justice and humanity for which American patriots sacrificed their lives and fortunes.

I, therefore, believe it is my duty to my country to love it; to support its constitution; to obey its laws; to respect its flag; and to defend it against all enemies.

Presented to Freddie Maggard with congratulations upon your high school graduation. May the future bring you success, happiness and achievement in the highest ideals of American citizenship.

Carl Perkins, Member of Congress
7th District, Kentucky

The Courier-Journal
1956 All-State Basketball Squad

This is to certify that FREDDIE MAGGARD, CARR CREEK High School, has been chosen for Third Team on The Courier-Journal All-State High School Basketball Squad, chosen by a Board made up of coaches, sports writers and officials in the Commonwealth of Kentucky.

Johnny Carrico, Chairman
Earl Ruby, All-State Committee Sports Editor

COMMONWEALTH OF KENTUCKY
Office of Lieutenant Governor
March 22, 1956

Mr. Freddie Maggard
Carr Creek, Ky.

Dear Freddie:

I want to take this opportunity of congratulations to you and your teammates on your fine performance during the state basketball tournament, and on the outstanding victory over all your opponents from the start to the final game of the tournament which crowned you champions for 1956.

As personal page to the Lieutenant Governor, and as a senior page of the Senate, I want to express great pride in having the Carr Creek basketball team as Kentucky's champions.

Sincerely yours,
Josh Kenton Lovelace, Jr.

Personal Page to the Lieutenant Governor,
Harry Lee Waterfield

COMMONWEALTH OF KENTUCKY
HOUSE OF REPRESENTATIVES

To All to Whom These Presents Shall Come, Greeting:

On Motion of Mr. Banjo Bill Cornett, of Knott County, Freddie Maggard was elected Honorary Page of the House of Representatives for the 1956 Regular Session.

Know Ye, that he having been duly elected Honorary Page is hereby vested with full power and authority to execute and discharge the duties of said office. And to have and to hold the same, with all the rights and emoluments thereunto legally appertaining, for and during the term prescribed.

Done at Frankfort, 21st day of
March in the year of our Lord one
thousand nine hundred and 56 and
in the one hundred and 64th year of the
Commonwealth.

Thomas P. Fitzpatrick, Speaker, House of Representatives
Jim Babbage, Chief Clerk, House of Representatives

"A RESOLUTION commending the Carr Creek basketball team upon the achievement in winning the 1956 Kentucky State High School Basketball Tournament."

Whereas, the basketball team of Carr Creek High School emerged victorious in the 1956 Kentucky State High School Basketball Tournament; and,

Whereas, this feat accomplished by the said Carr Creek team eliminating four other Kentucky high school basketball teams which furnished the best competition available; and

Whereas, the performance of the Carr Creek team reflected the highest credit upon the school which it represented and upon Kentucky high school basketball, not only in terms of technical proficiency but in a practical demonstration of sportsmanship; and

Whereas, it appears desirable that this honorable body join other citizens of the Commonwealth in honoring the achievement of the said Carr Creek basketball team,

NOW, THEREFORE,

Be it resolved by the Senate of the General Assembly of the Commonwealth of Kentucky:

Section I. That the Senate of the Commonwealth of Kentucky does hereby extend its expression of commendation to the basketball team of Carr Creek High School for its achievement in winning the 1956 Kentucky State High School Basketball Tournament.

Section II. That the Clerk of the Senate cause copies of this Resolution be sent to the County Superintendent of

Schools of Knott County, to the principal of Carr Creek High School and the coach and each of the players of the 1956 team.

HENDERSON HIGH SCHOOL
HONORARY AWARD

This certifies that Freddie Maggard of Carr Creek High School has been selected on the 1955-56 Henderson High School All-Opponent Team.

Congratulations on your outstanding play.

T. L. Plain, Coach
Byron Pinson and Pascal Benson, Team Captains

COMMONWEALTH OF KENTUCKY
Office of Lieutenant Governor

March 21, 1956

Dear Freddie:

I want to take this means of congratulating you and your teammates on your fine performance during the State Basketball Tournament, and the outstanding victory in the finals which crowned you Champions for 1956.

All Kentuckians take pride in having the Carr Creek basketball team as their champions.

Sincerely yours,

Harry Lee Waterfield
Lieutenant Governor

"It seems unusual, but Carr Creek's Freddie Maggard is receiving more publicity by not being selected on the All-Tournament Team than he would have if he had been picked. I don't think that I can remember the Kentucky State Senate passing a resolution that a player be an All-Stater, as was done by the Kentucky Senate Monday after Maggard was omitted. Frankly, I don't see how the experts left Maggard off. He did a terrific job in the tournament, hitting the winning goals in closing seconds of two of the games and averaging 15.5 points for the four games. I hope, however, that politics doesn't get into high school sports—though I do believe in this particular instance the Senate was correct in boosting the Carr Creek cager." (Billy Surface)

In 1956, the guard named Freddie Maggard rose to the heights of basketball stardom during the post-season tournament games. He was honored by most basketball coaches and awed by fans in the state of Kentucky for his outstanding play, leadership, and all-American personality.

After the champions returned home to Carr Creek to evaluate their whirlwind accomplishments and to check their mail, Freddie found he had twelve colleges writing offering full basketball scholarships. He finally chose Virginia

Polytechnic Institute (V.P.I.), and briefly enrolled before returning home to help his mother, Blanche Hylton Maggard (Mrs. Loyd) care for his terminally ill father, Loyd Maggard.

Freddie began to work as a surveyor. That seemed to be an easy job as his well-known lumber man grandfather, Jesse Hylton, had also been a successful surveyor. He soon left that job and took a position in the office of Blue Diamond Coal Mine #2 with a salary that afforded him the income to help his mother, Blanche, who had taken a job in the Carr Creek High School's lunchroom to maintain their standard of living so ably provided by Mr. Maggard.

At that time few students at Carr Creek High School worked after school or during summer break. So, Freddie provided the needed income to provide a high school education for his brother, Jesse Robert—named for grandfather Jesse Hylton—Bobbie Jean (Hicks), Betty Lou (Feltner), and Joyce (James)—"all graduated from Carr Creek High School, two at a time," stated Blanche. In remembering why he left college before getting a degree, or further possible basketball glories, Freddie stated, "I never even one time regretted returning home to Cody (one mile or so from the Carr Creek School) to help my Mom with an enormous burden to carry or to help provide for my brother and three sisters." This statement alone reflects the true Freddie Maggard.

Freddie Maggard is confident of his decision as oldest son to provide for his family; he is at peace with his personal commitment to God and dedication to his family. "Basketball taught me what I needed to do and to know how to make correct decisions," he reflects.

While at Blue Diamond Mine, Freddie found success and enjoyment. In 1957 he met Patricia ("Pat") Meade, "at work" in the same office. Pat Meade, a graduate of Leatherwood High School and a cheerleader, tells the story of listening to the 1956 state tournament and "yelling her head off for Freddie Maggard." Then in 1957 she met Freddie and they began dating. However, they did not marry until 1959. They later produced a pair of champions, Samantha (Burton), who teaches first grade at Williamsburg Elementary, Williamsburg, Kentucky; and Freddie Wayne II, former quarterback for the University of Kentucky Wildcats. While father, Freddie, excelled in basketball, "Freddie Jr." excelled in basketball, receiving honorable mention in Kentucky High School basketball and voted All-State in football! He received a full scholarship to play quarterback for the University of Kentucky. He was a success and wildly loved by the fans. He roomed for five years at U.K. with E. A. Couch's son, Joey, a Kentucky All-State offensive guard, with a full scholarship to the University of Kentucky to guard the Wildcats offensive line for Freddie Maggard II. They were and remain the best of friends, just as their fathers played and starred together for the Carr Creek High School 1956 Championship Team, and remain the best of friends.

In 1961, the United States Army sent Freddie Wayne Maggard an "invitation to join" (drafted) as a twenty-four year old. He was sent to Berlin, Germany, during the famous Berlin Crisis. That fire was extinguished and he next found himself in Guantanamo Bay, Cuba, helping to "put out another fire." Freddie remembers that "after Guantomo Bay— 1963—I returned to the states and was discharged." He said, "I returned to the Blue Diamond Coal Company and continued working in the office until my retirement as General Superintendent."

Then, Freddie, Patricia, Samantha, and Freddie II moved to Williamsburg, Kentucky (Whitley County), where he worked as manager of Teco Coal of Whitley County. He retired as Vice-President of Operations. Freddie Maggard used his intelligence, management skills, and superb personality to lead two large coal companies. He gives the Carr Creek High School faculty credit for his academic preparation for success.

Freddie was not without pain and distress while growing up, however. While in the eighth grade he fractured a leg in a farm accident that slowed his basketball development. Then an appendectomy compounded his slow development of becoming an early star for Carr Creek High School. These managed encounters gave him time to polish his skills of "if we can get away with it, let's try it" attitude. There are many stories being told of fun-loving Freddie's activities.

Freddie had an "old gray Plymouth," and he was the only boy on the basketball team with a car. Coach Morton Combs tells the story that "when I ordered a curfew for the team, I did not contact each player's home by driving by to check up on them—I just drove by Loyd Maggard's farm, and if the old gray Plymouth was parked, I would return home. If the car was not parked in front of the house, I knew that Freddie had the whole team out."

In recent years, Freddie has had to rely on his faith, his family, and the medical profession to see him through a light stroke, with complete recovery, and in 1999 a huge scare with a diagnosis of two cancerous polyps of the colon. He did well postoperatively from the removal of the two polyps. Freddie appreciates life!

Bobby Shepherd,
1956 Carr Creek Basketball Champion Center

Bobby Shepherd's parents moved to Carr Creek before "Bob" (as he is lovingly called) graduated from high school. This tall, handsome, bright young man was very welcome on Carr Creek Hill (the campus!). He was given the "old royal treatment"—especially by the basketball team as he was taller than any other player that would wear the blue and white come basketball season! Not only was Bobby Shepherd tall and strong, but he was a "rebounding machine." Without Bob we would not have the prized state basketball trophy as proof of the trip to Lexington and four days in Memorial Coliseum in March 1956. "Bob" graduated in May 1956, becoming a Creeker for life. He was given a full scholarship to the University of Kentucky to play basketball for the "Old Master," Adolph Rupp. (E. A. Couch, a graduating team-

mate of the 1956 team, was also given a full scholarship.)
Bob transferred after one year. Neither student athlete had
academic problems at the University of Kentucky.

The following is submitted by Bob Shepherd:

"After leaving the University of Kentucky, I attended
college one year at Tyler, Texas. Then I played basketball at
Lamar University at Beaumont, Texas, the next two years.
At Lamar, I was a member of the All-Conference team both
years and held the rebounding record for fifteen years.

"While I was at Lamar, I was married and became the father of a son, Michael. He is now a coach at Hughes Springs,
Texas. He has two sons and a daughter.

"I was married again some thirty years ago to my present wife, Martha, who taught English in the local school district. She retired two years ago. Our daughter, Kimberlie, is
a band director in the Spring Branch School District near
Houston. I also have a stepson, Jerry, who lives in Weather-
ford, Texas, where both he and his wife are teaching.

"After my senior year at Lamar, I went into sales, where
I have remained. It has been a challenging but rewarding
career.

"As I look back at the year I was at Carr Creek, I remember many things, especially my introduction to the
school. The introduction committee was headed by Freddie Maggard, who was assisted by Billy and Donald Hylton. They were to acquaint me with 'the campus.' We were
walking around the campus (hill) when hunger overtook us.

This prompted Freddie to open a cafeteria window, and we helped ourselves to crackers with cheese. A day or two later, there was a rumor circulating that someone had broken into the cafeteria.

"I also remember the interest, concern, and dedication of both Coach Combs and Coach Johnson. Coach Combs never seemed ruffled but was always in control. He had a look that his players 'knew well and understood.' Freddie will know what I'm talking about because he was sometimes the recipient of that look. Coach Johnson was always calm and cordial to the athletes.

"The community itself seemed involved with and a part of the team as they cheered and supported us."

Edward (Ed) Richardson, 1956 Carr Creek Basketball Champion Guard

Ed, as he is known to his family and friends, was raised near the headwaters of the Carr Creek Lake. He attended Carr Creek Elementary School, riding the school bus every day. In 1956, after the exciting championship basketball season, he graduated from Carr Creek High School in May. Before graduation, Ed was offered a basketball scholarship to play guard for Lees Junior College in Jackson, Kentucky. However, he chose to move to Louisville, where he gave General Electric Appliance Park in Louisville his attention for the next 35 years. In 1968, Edward Richardson married Phyllis Jackson, a professional nurse. She worked as a registered nurse at Jewish Hospital in Louisville primarily her entire career before retiring. Phyllis and Ed worked together to raise four happy, caring, close-knit Richardsons. All four are graduates of North Bullitt High School.

In November 1999, Ed came to a turning point—"a fork in the road"—in his life. He had open-heart surgery. He recovered on schedule—having a professional nurse in the home was reassuring and convenient during his recuperation. He is healthy once again. Ed enjoys daily walks, playing pool on his pool table at home, and challenging friends and family to a competitive game.

The University of Kentucky has a "True Blue Fan" in Ed Richardson. He rejoices when "his Cats" win and suffers when they lose. That is the essence of a True Blue Fan. Wonder if he does a little coaching from his favorite chair when the "Basketball Cats" take to the floor, especially monitoring guard play?

Baseball also gets the attention of sportsman Ed Richardson. He spends long summer hours watching his favorite team, the Cincinnati Reds, play baseball on television.

Today, Ed and Phyllis are retired and live in Shepherdsville, Kentucky. They are very appreciative of their health and family. They spend time enriching the lives of their four grandchildren while being close emotionally and literally (as neighbors) to their children.

Marcus Combs,
1956 Carr Creek Basketball Champion

"I am grateful that you are willing to take the time to write this book about the 1956 basketball team. I realize that Carr Creek had several great teams in their history. I feel we had the right team at the right time to bring the championship trophy back to the mountains.

"I was born December 1, 1936, to James Madison Combs and Maudie (Jent) Combs at Jeremiah, Kentucky. We moved to Red Fox, Kentucky, in 1940.

"I have one brother, Lawrence C. Combs, who lives at Red Fox, Kentucky, and four sisters, Imojean Travis, Juanita Soards, Alta Mae Freeman, all in Marion, Indiana, and Helen Collins, Summitville, Indiana.

"I married Lydia Mac Maddin, the daughter of Odis Elmer Maddin and Goldie (Combs) Maddin, on May 18, 1956, at Jeremiah, Kentucky. Lydia and I have four children: two sons, Marcus Anthony Combs of Marion, Indiana, who married Denise Soards . . . [and] also Maurice Allen Combs of Lexington, Kentucky, who married Amy Rodeheaver. We also have two daughters: Deborah Jean Mullins and Dinah June Stanley, who married Bruce Stanley.

"I worked in several places for the first four years after high school: Hamilton, Ohio; Chicago, Illinois; Cleveland, Ohio; and Detroit, Michigan. Then in 1960 I came to Marion, Indiana.

"I was employed for General Motors for 30.2 years and

retired in July 1990. I held several classifications while employed for GM—production, shipping inspector, quality control, and salvage repairman.

"My mother, Maudie Combs, was killed in a car accident at Jeff, Kentucky, on March 18, 1966. The odd thing about that is that John C. Mullins, whom I roomed with when we were on roads trips and while we were at the state tournament at Lexington, was killed at the same place. Needless to say, it still hurts to think about it.

"I took an interest in basketball at a very young age, about four years old. I took an old leather lace-up basketball that didn't have a bladder in it and filled it full of rags. We used a bushel basket nailed to the side of the house for a goal.

"I attended Breedings Creek Grade School where Zelda Hale was a teacher for many years. Mr. Hale taught us the fundamentals of playing basketball; then it was onto Carr Creek Grade School and Carr Creek High School.

"Winning the state championship is one of the great thrills of my life. Leaving out of the mountains and going to the big city of Lexington was, to me, like leaving out of the U.S.A. When we met to eat lunch in the motel there were sixteen teams. After the first round there was eight, then four, two, then just Carr Creek. The last meal was several platters filled with large, rare steaks with the trimmings.

"Returning back to Hazard and seeing the people lining the road for miles and the team riding on the fire truck back to the Courthouse and thousands of people gathered to celebrate the team's victory was just too much for a country boy.

"I came under conviction for my sins really good in 1969 and was born into God's glorious family in September 1971. Two years later I realized that God had called me to preach his gospel. After exercising my gift for several years, I became an ordained minister on November 12, 1977 at the Northern Little Dove Church of the Old Regular Baptist in Sidney, Indiana. After serving a short time as Assistant Pastor, we planted a new church in Marion, Indiana, named the Lydia Baptist Church. I have pastored the Lydia Baptist Church since August 1981.

"Some of the privileges I have had in the many years of serving the Lord are writing the circular letter to the Indian Bottom Association and a year later being picked by the Indian Bottom Association to preach the introductory sermon. I have had the privilege of seeing many, many souls born into God's family and baptized.

"I will be forever grateful to the precious memories of growing up in the mountains of southeastern Kentucky; for the teachers who taught us not only the necessary subjects in class, but instilled in us the desire to be successful in life."

Estill Adams,
1956 Carr Creek Basketball Champion Guard

Estill Adams is a Carr Creek "Valley Boy," having been "borned" across the valley from the Carr Creek Hill, on

December 29, 1938. He was raised on a small farm by the big wide creek called "the Singing Carr." He was always within sight of the old limestone high school building on "the hill." His parents, James ("Jim") and Bonnie (Franklin) Adams, were loved and respected by the Carr Creek community. By living so close to Carr Creek Elementary and Carr Creek High School, they assured their children—Sarah, Nell, Betty, Cecil, Estill, and Lorraine—of never having to board a school bus to get to school and never missing basketball practice, cheerleading practice, or a school play practice. They raised a beautiful, involved family that took academics seriously.

While the Adams Farm is now covered by the Carr Creek Lake, Estill draws comfort from the beautiful lake as he drives by each day on his way to work for Kentucky Processing Company (which processes coal for consumer use).

Estill graduated from Carr Creek High School in May 1958. He has been married to Nancy Reynolds Adams—a local girl—for 34 years. They are the parents of Kimisu and James. Estill's daughter Kim is a teacher, lives in Perry County, and is the mother of three beautiful children. Son James resides in Somerset with his wife, Mary, and has two precious children. Estill has been a devoted father and now is a doting grandparent. His children are amazed at his "inherent gentleness" and his enjoyment of the simple things in life. Estill Adams, Carr Creek guard on the championship team, is now a master gardener and is known throughout the Carr Creek area for his ability to attract the elusive hummingbirds to his feeders. These gentle little birds, recognizing "naturalist Estill" as their friend, will even light on his fingers. Could it be they sense his gentle spirit? The local deer population depend on "naturalist Estill" to feed them bags of corn during the bleak winter season. They, too, seem to have no fear of this "gentle Creeker," as they will walk right up and almost eat out of his hands!

Estill Adams is today a concerned environmentalist. This is probably secondary to the Adams farm being covered by the Carr Creek Lake, while strip mining runoff and development has changed the early environment of the unspoiled hills and creeks. The Carr Creek Lake is much healthier today, with swimming, fishing, boating, and water skiing being enjoyed in summer by "Creekers" and tourists.

Estill is a contented man, enjoying his "near the lake" home. Estill Adams reflects on the championship game in Memorial Coliseum in 1956. He states: "Every young basketball player should have the experience of the thrill of winning the Sweet Sixteen, as me and my teammates did." He says that "it was a privilege to have played and won the game that brought the crown home to Carr Creek Hill."

Sidney ("Sid") Adams, a brother of "Jim" Adams, drove one of Carr Creek's school buses. He would have been the driver to pick up his nieces and nephews, but they chose to walk—not having to meet Uncle Sid's schedule.

Sid Adams, loved by all of the students at Carr Creek High School, as well as the elementary school, was also the "bus driver" for many of the basketball teams. He drove the bus on "road trips" when necessary and became an important part of the Carr Creek legacy.

Ray Stamper,
1956 Carr Creek Basketball Champion Forward

Ray Stamper played forward for the 1956 Carr Creek State Basketball Champions. "He was a big, strong, intelligent ball player," remembers Coach Morton Combs. It has been said that Ray Stamper had "the genetic stuff" to play basketball well. He was a first cousin of the famous Shelby Stamper, Carr Creek's 1928 High School All-American, who was also a forward. While Ray had ten players on the 1956 champion team, Shelby was one of five that played the entire season. However, the 1928 Carr Creek Community Center's team had eight boys on the squad. Ray Stamper has another cousin that was a starting guard for Carr Creek's 1948 state tournament team that placed third, Wiley B. Stamper. The three basketball players were sons of brothers.

Ray states that when Carr Creek won the championship that night in Memorial Coliseum, Lexington, Kentucky, "I did not realize the importance of what we had done." The excitement was too much for most mountain boys to absorb in one evening. The thrill of it all—big book-smart Ray Stamper tried to analyze what it all meant, and that he had come to the end of his basketball journey.

Ray graduated from Carr Creek in May 1956. He attended Caney Creek Junior College (now Alice Lloyd College),

Pippapasses, Kentucky, for two years. Mrs. Lloyd, being impressed with Ray's academic potential, sent him to the University of Kentucky to complete a Bachelor of Science degree. He lived in the Caney Cottage just off campus with Mrs. Lloyd's scholars. Mrs. Lloyd sent the best and brightest to live in her cottage—free room, board, and education of choice, subtly approved by Mrs. Lloyd, President of Caney Creek Junior College, of course. Ray and his fellow "Caney scholars" walked to their classes, ate, slept, and studied—sometimes pulling all-nighters, it has been said.

Ray Stamper proved to be an apt student, carrying a double major at the University of Kentucky in Biological Science and History. He graduated from the University of Kentucky in two years prepared to be a scholar teacher. He taught biological sciences in a large high school in Ohio for a few years before returning to his Carr Creek Lake home to care for his aging, ill mother until her death.

Today, Ray lives less than one mile from the lake and cares for his hobby vegetable garden in the summer. The remainder of this intelligent Creeker's time is spent reading—"I read anything and everything," states Ray.

One day in August 1999, we had the pleasure of meeting Ray Stamper—visiting on the front porch of his home, and thinking we were disturbing him at 8 a.m. on that bright, sunny morning. But he assured us that he had been out of bed for hours, reading. We were there to discuss his memories of what being a Carr Creek ball player and graduate had meant to him; what he had majored in at the University of

Kentucky. A wide range of topics were quickly covered, and suddenly he mentioned "Robert E. Lee, the poorest of warriors and one of the brightest," and right then the historian superceded the scientist. He has a strong feeling for history and is noted for his in-depth reading of the Civil War.

Ray Stamper continues to read and grow as a scholar, yet his Carr Creek Lake relatives and neighbors revere him for his simple way of living and his knowledgeable thinking.

John C. Mullins

John C. Mullins (1937-1989) is lovingly remembered by his sister Beulah Mae Mullins Ashley (Mrs. Luther Ashley). Beulah Mae ("Boots") graduated from Carr Creek in May 1950. My wife, Sue Watts Miller, graduated in the same class, and she and Boots are still very close friends (and cousins).

The following information is Mrs. Ashley's comments about her brother.

"John C. Mullins was born on February 27, 1937, to Charlie and Sarah Fields Mullins at Amburgey, Kentucky. He lived at Amburgey his entire life.

"He grew up in a large family—four brothers and four sisters. At an early age he learned to help with chores such as working on hillside cornfields."

(See, I wasn't the only one hoeing corn on a hillside, feeding the farm animals, and keeping the woodbox filled.)

"Education was very important to John from early childhood. He attended Upper Trace Fork Elementary School and walked two miles each morning to catch a bus to Carr Creek High School. He enjoyed playing basketball for Carr Creek even though he had to walk two miles back home in the dark—good or bad weather—after ball practice as well as after ball games.

"John C. graduated from Carr Creek in May 1956, after his exciting championship tournament in the Memorial Coliseum, Lexington, Kentucky. He continued his education at Lee's Junior College, Jackson, Kentucky. After he graduated from Lees Junior College, he immediately enrolled at Eastern Kentucky University (his beloved E.K.U.), Richmond, Kentucky. John C. was an education major, and each summer he attended graduate classes from E.K.U. at Little Buckhorn in Perry County.

"One summer three ladies that he knew were also taking classes from E.K.U. at Little Buckhorn, so they took turns driving their cars. One day, one of the female students had a flat tire and did not have a lug bolt wrench, so one of them suggested John C. walk down the road to a garage to borrow the needed lug bolt wrench. In the meantime, a motorist stopped and fixed the flat tire. They drove on to pick up John and while going around a curve, they saw John sitting on a big rock by the side of the road. They asked him what he was doing sitting there waiting and he said, 'I knew someone would stop and change the tire for you!'

"John C.'s first teaching job was in a one-room school on Patton Fork in Knott County. To reach the school he had to walk over a mountain. He boarded with the parents of one of his students through the week, and his brother-in-law (Luther Ashley) would go to get him on Friday evening and take him back on Sunday afternoon. He also taught elementary education at the Big Smith Branch School at Smithsboro. He later took a position at the Emmalena Elementary School when it opened and taught there until he and his wife were killed in an automobile accident in May 1989. He would have retired from teaching in two weeks.

"John C. and Lillie were killed on the day of the annual Carr Creek High School reunion, always on Memorial Day weekend. The accident and subsequent deaths were announced over the intercom to the "gathered Creekers," and people immediately began to remember the strong personalities they shared, and their devotion to their family.

"John C. and Lillie Mae Whitaker married in 1960. Lillie Mae was a graduate of Carr Creek High School. She and John C. were the proud parents of Doyle, Alan, and Stacy.

"When they died, they were on their way to Hazard to shop for a graduation gift for Stacy, a soon-to-be graduate of Knott County Central High School. After picking up Stacy's gift, they were planning on attending the Carr Creek Reunion in the old gymnasium on Carr Creek Hill, but Doyle relates that 'they only reached Jeff, Kentucky—almost there . . .' Their children continue to live near the Carr Creek Lake.

"John C. was a much-loved and devoted teacher. His belief in education and devotion to his students set an example for many young lives. He spent many years as a baseball and basketball coach, worked with the Carr Creek Head Start Program for several summers, and was an active member of the Carr Creek Lions Club.

"John C. had the respect of the faculty as well as the students of Emmalena Elementary. One of the teachers told his family that if a teacher had playground duty and had an unruly child that was difficult to manage, they would send for John. He would come and take the child aside and talk to that child. After a conversation with John C., the child would behave for the rest of the day. She said, 'I would like to have known what he might have said to that child.'

"This 'boy of Irishman Creek,' never having lived any other place except when in college, loved 'this place' that provided the mountains and promoted his love of nature. He never outgrew his love of nature, and a favorite pasttime was to pack a picnic lunch and spend a day exploring with his family."

Donald Guy Combs,
Carr Creek Basketball Team Manager

Donald was a manager for the 1956 State Champions, "a true Creeker" who continues to be amazed at the success of his small high school battling the titans of our Commonwealth.

Donald graduated from Carr Creek High School in May 1956. He enrolled that fall at Cumberland Junior College, Williamsburg, Kentucky, as an elementary education major.

He completed two years at the junior college and returned to Perry County to begin teaching elementary school in Scuddy Hollow. He spent the first six summers after graduating from Cumberland Junior College attending Eastern State University at Richmond, Kentucky. So, for six years, after leaving the old limestone building on Carr Creek Hill, he taught for nine months and spent the summer at Eastern State University. Then, he left teaching to take a more lucrative job in the coal industry, as he had a growing family to care for.

The coal industry kept Donald's attention for the next 30 years. He enjoyed his work, raising his three boys and two girls. Donald Guy married the beautiful, vivacious Hazel Burnett of Vicco, Kentucky, in 1957. They always have big discussions on the comparison between Vicco (consolidated into Dilce Combs Memorial) and Carr Creek basketball.

Donald and Hazel settled in the Lothair section of Hazard, Kentucky, where they raised Donald Gene, Ronald Dean, and Ricky Layne. Then along came two possible cheerleaders—Robin Renee and Rhonda Kaye. However, only Robin Renee was a Hazard High School cheerleader, while Rhonda Kaye played basketball on the Hazard High School girls' team. Ronald Dean played basketball for Hazard High during his four years. The sports influence Donald had on his children was certainly an advantage for Hazard High School.

While Donald and Hazel's five children are true Perry Countians, we must remember that Perry Countians have a long history of being loyal to Carr Creek High School basketball teams since 1928, when the Perry County schools were not in the fray.

Donald Guy Combs, a forever Creeker at heart, retired in the late eighties, and has been in another battle for the last five years: mini-stroke syndrome. The small strokes have left him with some impairment, as he was forced to go on total disability, but he is able to attend most athletic games of his grandchildren. He is a big fan of most sports, and "pulls time" in front of his television set. He is a man with a positive attitude who makes the most of his time: enjoying his family and his best friend, Hazel.

Donald is a nephew of Gurney Adams, Carr Creek's famous 1928 point guard. He and Gurney and Mary Adams's daughter, Shirley Adams Sizemore (Mrs. Douglas Sizemore, Lexington, Kentucky) thrive on their genetic connection. He grew up visiting and playing on the Carr Creek Hill. He remembers visiting the "Patchwork Cottage" that the Adamses have owned all of their married life (now Shirley, the only heir, is the loving caretaker). The "Patchwork Cottage" was one of the first cottages built for the Carr Creek Community Center for Miss Weston and Miss Marsh, teacher-administrators for the first school. It was built of discarded lumber, doors, and windows. It is now a lovely white cottage among the green pines on the Carr Creek Hill Road.

Donald ("Donnie") Hylton
Carr Creek Basketball Team Manager

"Donnie" was one of two managers for the 1956 State Champion Carr Creek team. He "often drives to Carr Creek Hill to look around and remember what a joy and a surprise it was to actually win the championship—to beat all of these large schools, and win it all!" He states, "I felt a part of the team, as one of the managers—everyone did." He added, "I am so proud to be a graduate of Carr Creek High School (1956), as is my wife, Charlene" (Charlene Gumon of Letcher County, Class of 1958).

Donnie further states that his family—the Clyde Hylton Family—farm is now under the Carr Creek Lake, about one mile from the Carr Creek Hill. He says he drives by that area each day on his way to work in Yellow Creek (Knott County) at Florida Power Coal, shipping coal by train to the Crystal River Power Plant in Florida.

When talking to Donald Hylton one gets the feeling that driving to the old limestone high school building on Carr Creek Hill is the only way he can "go home."

While Donnie began to work in the mining industry soon after graduating in 1956 from his beloved Carr Creek High School, he needed an excuse to stay conveniently close to Charlene, who did not graduate until May 1958.

Donald Hylton and Charlene Gumon married as soon as Charlene received her diploma, becoming a "Creeker."

They began their family of three daughters: Delania, Denise, and Deanne.

Delania (Mrs. Randy Fields) graduated from Whitesburg High School and Letcher County Vocational School. She is employed by the Pike Community Bank of Whitesburg. She actively promotes her husband Randy's employment with Coastal Coal Company. They live in Whitesburg, Kentucky.

Denise (Mrs. Byron Jacob) graduated from Whitesburg High School, Alice Lloyd College (a junior college at that time), and Morehead State University. She is now teaching at Alice Lloyd College, continues taking graduate courses, and promotes her husband's banking career. She has produced three Jacobs: Brynann Nicole and identical twin boys, Conner and Colton.

Dianne (Mrs. Jimmy Collins) graduated from Whitesburg High School, Alice Lloyd, and Morehead State University. She teaches in the Knott County School System and lives in the Hindman, Kentucky area. She is a counselor at Knott Central High School and "attends basketball games," as her husband is the coach of the boys' basketball team.

The delighted manager of the 1956 State Champions is a now breeder of beagle dogs and raises miniature horses. "I have always loved dogs," he states. "The miniature horses are for the three grandchildren." Donnie, as busy Charlene calls him, spends Saturdays with his grandchildren as they ride "their horses" and with his beagle dogs. He has become a loving, dedicated grandfather.

Donald Hylton is a proud, contented Creeker living less than ten miles "from home," the lake and Carr Creek Hill.

Richard Douglas ("Rick") Johnson, 1956 Carr Creek Basketball Champions Mascot

Richard ("Rick") Johnson is "a product of the Carr Creek Hill." He grew up on the hill and completed Carr Creek Elementary School and Carr Creek High School, graduating in May 1965.

Once "Rick" completed his schooling on the hill, he enrolled at the University of Kentucky, majoring in Political Science, and graduated in 1969 with a Bachelor of Arts in Political Science. Kentucky Senator Douglas "Doug" Hays, his maternal grandfather, influenced young Rick to appreciate the political process. After graduating from the University of Kentucky, he entered the military service: from 1969-71 he was in the United States Army, 2nd Lieutenant Infantry Division. He was discharged after completing two years and enrolled at Eastern Kentucky University (E.K.U.) in the fall of 1971. Before beginning work on his Master of Arts at E.K.U., Rick spent some time on Carr Creek Hill that summer, getting his mind and soul ready for the academic challenge.

In 1973, Rick began his banking career at First Security Bank of Lexington, later to be known as Bank One, Main Street, Lexington, Kentucky. He has worked in Systems and Operations for both banks, where he continues today.

Rick had a big year in 1973: he began his banking career and married Karen Flood, a teacher, in May. That would prove to be a "comfort zone" for him, as he already knew how to "manage teachers": his parents, Willard "Sprout" Johnson (coach) and Nelle (Hays), were teachers.

Karen Flood Johnson taught school in Louisville, Jefferson County, Kentucky, and in the Fayette County Public Schools as a special education teacher for 28 years before retiring in 1998. She is busy as wife of Rick and mother for two former University of Kentucky students: daughter Brooke and son Todd.

Brooke Elizabeth, born July 20, 1977, is a 1995 graduate of Henry Clay High School. In the fall she enrolled at the University of Kentucky as a pre-law student, graduating in June 1999. She was accepted by the University of Kentucky's School of Law in the fall of 1999. Todd Owen came bounding into the hearts of Rick, Karen, and the Johnsons from Carr Creek Hill on April 13, 1980. Todd graduated from Henry Clay High School in June 1999, enrolled at the University of Kentucky in the fall of 1999, and worked on his goal of becoming an Air Force pilot.

To Rick Johnson, the Carr Creek Hill is home. From cradle to college and beyond, he has called "home" one of the original log cabins that was built for an early Carr Creek Community Center Director, Margaret Humes. His parents, Willard "Sprout" and Nelle, purchased the log cabin from Miss Humes when she left, after 12 years of educational service. The unique log cabin was christened "Happy Log" by the Johnsons. As Rick Johnson goes home today, he drives by the Carr Creek Lake, up the "Hill Road," and makes a soft right turn at the crest of the hill onto "Happy Log Lane," a hemlock tree-lined drive. The entrance to this memorable drive has an original, cozy, flower-bedecked cottage on it, the home of sister Ann and husband, Denver Pratt. The shaded "Happy Log Lane" goes by another original log cabin built for Carr Creek Community Center's "Miss Raney." The peacefulness of the woods, wildlife—squirrels darting here and everywhere—and the blue water of what once was called "the singing Carr" is home to Rick Johnson.

Glen Combs, 1956 Carr Creek Basketball Champions Mascot

One of Morton's joys was getting to coach his son, Glen. Though Glen was a good player at Carr Creek, he still was not strong his first three years, but it was another story, when he became a senior. With added strength and maturity, he became outstanding and was voted the outstanding player in the 14th Region his senior year. He received a full basketball scholarship at Virginia Tech.

Glen was outstanding in college at Tech. He was on Tech's team that defeated Indiana University in the NCAA at Chicago in 1967, only to be defeated by Dayton in an overtime, which would have put Tech in the Final Four.

In 1986, Glen had the honor to be selected on the first five of the five best all-time teams at Virginia Tech. He is

Tech's third all-time leading scorer, and in 1987 he was elected to the Athletic Hall of Fame at Tech.

After Glen's graduation, he turned professional. He was selected by the Utah team in the American Basketball Association. He was the leading scorer for Utah for approximately six or seven years. Then, the American Basketball Association merged with the National Basketball Association and the team was called the Utah Jazz. He played well in the NBA for a few years and then injured his knee and had to retire. He is married to Marsha McNiel of Roanoke, Virginia. They have two sons, Brian and Christopher.

Brian graduated from the University of Virginia. He obtained a MBA at Wake Forest University and is a very successful banker in Richmond, Virginia. Christopher (Chris) received a full football scholarship to Duke University. He graduated in December 1999 and was a hard-nosed lineman. He was chosen to play in the Senior Bowl in January 2000. In the fall of 2000 Chris signed a contract for the Pittsburgh Steelers.

Carr Creek High School's gymnasium, where the Indians practiced for their championship games.

The 1956 championship team. Top row (L-R): Assistant Coach Willard Johnson, Estill Adams, Ed Richardson, E. A. Couch, John C. Mullins, Warren Amburgey, Freddie Maggard, Bob Shepherd, Marcus Combs, Ray Stamper, Jim Calhoun, Head Coach Morton Combs. Bottom row (L-R): Manager Donald Hilton; Cheerleaders Peggy Collins, Christine Reedy, Polly Mullins, Captain Jane Calhoun, Nora Jean Hamilton; Manager Donald Combs. (Not pictured: Mascots Rick Johnson and Glen Combs)

Willard "Sprout" Johnson, assistant coach. He was on the squad of the 1948 Carr Creek team, and he coached two all-state players, Bill Morton and Don Miller.

Mr. Morton Combs, principal and head basketball coach of Carr Creek High School. He was chosen as one of the 26 charter inductees in the Kentucky High School Athletic Association Hall of Fame and was voted Kentucky's coach of the year in 1963.

Carr Creek cheerleaders rally the team at the state tournament. (L-R) Peggy Collins, Nora Hamilton, and Christine Reedy. The little "wannabe cheerleader" is Glenna Combs.

Warren G. Amburgey was a terror on the floor. Here he blocks out #66, Kelly Coleman of Wayland, in a tremendous game won by Carr Creek on a last-second shot by Freddie Maggard.

Freddie Maggard (27) gets a ride from his teammates after his last-second winning shot to beat Wayland by one point in the 1956 state semifinals. The players below (L-R) are Bobby Shepherd, Marcus Combs, Ed Richardson, Jim Calhoun (29), and E. A. Couch (33).

The championship trophy is held by Carr Creekers after their 72–68 win over Henderson at Lexington's Coliseum. In front of the team are Rickey Johnson, left, age 9, and Glen Combs, also age 9.

The victory swagger: E. A. Couch, Freddie Maggard, and Jim Calhoun, Blue Bird Mining Company, Anco, Kentucky, boys, after returning from the state championship. The house to the right is a miner's boarding house. Middle left is a railroad leading to a mining tipple just right of Maggard. A mining cemetery is in the background to the left of Couch's head.

8

Their Cheerleaders

The 1956 Carr Creek Champions had five cheerleaders to "cheer" them to victory: Jane Carolyn Calhoun (Couch), Peggy Lynn Collins (Hopper), Polly Geraldine Mullins (Merritt), Nora Jean Hamilton (Bentley), and Christine Reedy (Godsey).

To be a Carr Creek cheerleader had absolutely nothing to do with years of gymnastics training. It was all heart, beauty, and personality (not necessarily in that order). One had to at least be, if not beautiful, which so many were, in possession of the skills of a gifted politician. It was imperative that "the electorate," the students of both the elementary and high schools, be acquainted—yes, even love—"the candidate." The girl that set her heart on being elected to the cheering squad began "her campaign" on the Old Indian

Gathering Ground in front of the high school on the first day of any given school year. The candidate was required to have a strong academic point standing, to be of strong moral character, and to be in "the good graces" of the faculty because they possessed subtle influence on the voters. It was an honor to be elected to the Carr Creek Cheerleading Squad.

The 1956 Championship Cheerleaders were also very strong academic students. Two of the five were high school scholars.

Jane Carolyn Calhoun

Jane Carolyn Calhoun (Couch) graduated in 1956 after cheering for her Indians for four years. While "Janie" cheered with her heart, she was also a friend of all of the cheerleaders and ball players. Yet she never forgot the voters that had duly elected her for four years. She remains a popular Creeker.

Jane Calhoun never even one time slacked off on her academic responsibilities while cheerleading. She was the valedictorian of the 1956 graduating class—a solid 4.0—enrolled at Berea College in the fall of 1956, and completed her freshman year before marrying E. A. Couch, a star on the championship squad of 1956. Then she transferred to the University of Kentucky for her sophomore year, continuing her scholarship studies.

When her husband E. A. transferred from the University of Kentucky to the University of Dayton, Jane also transferred to the University of Dayton, graduating with a 3.9 point standing.

Jane Carolyn Calhoun (Couch) was in the throes of the busiest time of her young life. She was a wife, young mother, and a scholarship student trying to find time to excel in all areas. Before moving with E. A., young David, and Joey to Paintsville, Kentucky, she obtained her Master of Arts from Bowling Green University, Sandusky, Ohio. She majored in English and counseling with a 4.0 academic standing.

After establishing a new home in Paintsville, Kentucky, Jane began taking classes at Morehead State University, evenings and summer terms, to earn the Rank I in Education. She again graduated with a lofty 4.0.

Jane has had a busy career, and it reflects the preparation of a scholar. For the last several years, she has been an honored counselor for Johnson County Schools, Paintsville, Kentucky. Jane is also a recognized poet, having been inducted into the Kentucky Arts Council in 1976 as a poet, at the Galt House in Louisville, Kentucky. She is a very dedicated musician, too, the organist for the First Baptist Church, Paintsville, Kentucky, for years. She has had an illustrious career as teacher and counselor, but she is now eager to allow more time for family, especially E. A. and sons David and Joey, and their families. She will continue to find her own scholarly path to contentment.

Peggy Lynn Collins

Peggy Lynn Collins (Hopper), a popular cheerleader for the 1956 Champions, certainly had the "criteria" of a Carr Creek cheerleader. It has been said of Peggy Lynn that she had beauty, intelligence, and self-pride (Sue Watts Miller). Peggy Lynn describes her Carr Creek roots below.

"After watching several of my cousins graduate from Carr Creek High, I was more than ready for my turn. At that time, my one goal in life was to be a Carr Creek cheerleader. I was elected my sophomore year and needless to say, in my mind, I had it made. That year and the next three were wonderful years and I shall cherish them always. Being a part of that championship season and team will always be one of the most memorable times in my life.

"After graduation, I attended Cumberland Junior College in Williamsburg, Kentucky, 1956-59. While there, I was active in many student and campus organizations. I was elected Homecoming Queen in 1957 and was a member of the Student Government Council. At that time, I was planning to continue my education and teach.

"After leaving Cumberland, I came back to Hazard and went to work as a secretary at General Motors Acceptance Corporation. I had met Winston, my husband, during high school but we didn't start dating until 1958 and we were married in 1961. Winston is a "Hazard boy" and to this day we still have many heated discussions over some of the Hazard–Carr Creek basketball games. He attended Eastern and decided in 1980 to try college again and entered Jefferson State here in Birmingham.

"After marriage, we moved to Leesburg, Florida. Our twin daughters, Robin and Renee, were born there in 1962. Winston worked in the citrus business and I was a stay-at-home mom. When Robin and Renee started school, I accepted a job as a legal secretary. Winston, by this time, was Sales Manager for Ditch Witch Trenchers of Florida, Inc. I was quite active during those years in Leesburg doing volunteer work for the children's school and especially for Harry Anna Crippled Children's Home.

"In 1976, the opportunity presented itself for us to purchase a Ditch Witch dealership, which happened to be in Pelham, Alabama (just outside Birmingham). We formed Hopper Equipment Co., Inc., and purchased Ditch Witch of North Alabama. Winston and I ran the corporation and the business until we sold it in 1980.

"Robin and Renee graduated from high school in 1980. Robin attended Auburn University at Montgomery and graduated in 1984 with a degree in Criminal Justice. She worked as a paralegal for several years and is now in human resources. Renee attended the University of North Alabama but found other things to do and never finished. She is married and has given us three grandchildren.

"After selling the business, I went back to work as a legal secretary and continue working today. I am still involved in various civic organizations and do volunteer work for Children's Hospital here in Birmingham. Winston is now semi-retired and we recently purchased a small farm just outside London, Kentucky, where one day we hope to retire. But at the present time, with my work, volunteer work, and grand-children, I am a very busy and happy lady. Life is good.

"Now, what does Carr Creek mean to me? Carr Creek means home. A safe haven to go to where you are accepted just for being you and for the simple fact you are a 'Carr Creeker.' The teachers gave me the confidence and ability to go do what I wanted with my life. I never thought of myself as 'a poor country girl from Sassafras.' I was a graduate of Carr Creek, and I had a place in this world. All I had to do was go find it—and I did."

Polly Geraldine Mullins

The following is by Polly Geraldine Mullins herself, with additional statements by Sue Watts Miller.

"My name is Polly Geraldine Mullins (Mrs. Ronald Carl Merritt), born in Litt Carr, Kentucky, to Spencer and Gladys Mullins. I am the second oldest of seven children.

"I attended grades one through eight at Yellow Creek Elementary and nine through twelve at Carr Creek High School.

"One of the highlights of my junior and senior years was being a cheerleader for the Carr Creek Indians, who went to State in 1956 and won the championship.

"After graduating in 1957, I was hired at AT&T, Cincinnati, Ohio, where I worked for approximately six months.

"I met my husband, Ronald Carl Merritt, through mutual friends. We were married in 1959. We had two children: a boy (Keith) and a girl (Rhonda). I chose to stay home and raise my children.

"After ten years, I decided to go back to work and was employed by the Cincinnati Bell Telephone Company as a telephone operator. Six years later, I was promoted to a Supervisor. In 1980, I was promoted to Manager of Communications.

"I attended Southern Ohio College from 1981 to 1983, majoring in Business Management. I retired from Cincinnati Bell in 1985, after 15 years of employment.

"We lived in Ohio until 1991, when we decided to purchase an additional home in Florida. We commute back and forth every six months.

"I became a grandma in 1984, 1988, and 1998. Daughter Rhonda Kelly Merritt is the mother of Kelly Marie Speckert (17) and Gregory Ray Speckert, Jr. (12). Son Keith and wife, Dawn, are the doting parents of two-year-old Sean Keith Merritt.

Geraldine told the story of the cheerleaders staying in the Phoenix Hotel in Lexington, Kentucky, during the 1956 state tournament. They (the cheerleaders) had their "support team," headed by "B" team cheerleader, Imogene Francis Watts, sleeping on the floor (if this wild, fun-loving group of bright "young Creekers" ever slept), sleeping across the two beds, or draped over the chairs. The cheerleaders and their "support system" ate, walked, talked, and "toured Lexington on foot" when not busy in Memorial Coliseum cheering for their Indians.

Geraldine remembers how she dressed daughter Rhonda Kelly Merritt for a high school "1950s Hop" as a Carr Creek cheerleader. She wore her mom's cheerleading sweater—royal blue with the large white "C"—her royal blue skirt lined with white satin, white socks, and black-and-white saddle oxfords. The experience was heart-tugging for young Rhonda.

For years Rhonda and brother Keith have literally "played Santa Claus" for the present Carr Creek Elementary School at Christmas, making sure that the disadvantaged children get a gift to take home. Their friends and work associates help with money to buy gifts, or buy and wrap gifts, for the children. Polly Geraldine always sends a check from she and Ronald for her sister Deborah Mullins, counselor for Carr Creek Elementary, to buy what is needed for an especially poor child. Thus, Geraldine has involved her heart and the hearts of her two children in the continuing love and respect for the place called "Carr Creek."

Nora Jean Hamilton

Nora Jean Hamilton (Bentley) was elected to cheer for her Indians in the fall of her senior year. Nora Jean, a soft-spoken, dark-eyed beauty and an excellent student, was one of the five cheerleaders on the 1956 cheerleading squad. She was the one that chose to stay home after graduating in May

1956. Nora Jean married a handsome, young student who had transferred to Carr Creek High School from Wayland High School (Wayland, Kentucky), Noah Bentley. They were engaged during the 1956 school year and were married two weeks post-graduation. They lived and raised their family within one mile of the Carr Creek Lake. She stayed home with her children for eight years.

In 1965, Nora Jean became Chief Clerk of the Corp of Engineers Real Estate Project Office in Hindman, Kentucky. Their duty was to secure land for the Carr Creek Lake Project. Once again, she continued to be a strong and loyal advocate of Carr Creek.

Then in 1971, the Corp. of Engineers, as the Dam and Lake Project became known at Carr Creek, closed their office, leaving Nora Jean to scurry around looking for a job in an area where few jobs were available. It was just about that time when Noah, a supervisor for the Knott, Letcher, and Perry Counties Independent Coal Operators Association, changed jobs and needed a secretary for his new office. So, Nora Jean became head secretary for the Director, Noah, of Self Insurance Fund for Coal Miners, where she continues to work today.

Nora Jean, with Noah's help, has made a "hobby" of looking after and "troubleshooting" for beloved Creekers everywhere. She continues to keep an updated roster of former faculty and students, especially the 1956 class, basketball team, and cheering squad. She has kept in touch with them and has been a base of reference for them. She never tires of being available to the Creekers who have moved away and find themselves without their friends' locations and telephone numbers.

Nora Jean and her "adopted Creeker," Noah, have raised three "purebred Creekers."

Beverly Bentley (Perkins) attended Carr Creek High School for three years and was a member of the first graduating class of the new consolidated high school, Knott County Central, Hindman, Kentucky. She married and left to work in real estate in Dayton, Ohio.

Brenda Bentley (McPeeks) lives near the Carr Creek Lake. She graduated from Knott Central High School, Morehead State University (B.A.), and Eastern Kentucky State University (M.A.) and continues to earn graduate hours above the Masters degree. She strives to be the very best teacher of English for her Knott Central High School students. She is very dedicated to her mountain students and enjoys caring for her two boys near her Carr Creek Lake home.

"J. J." (John Jefferson) Bentley graduated from Knott Central High School and attended Eastern Kentucky University in Richmond, Kentucky. He has been trained in Foods Management and is a supervisor for a dining room in Richmond, Kentucky.

Nora Jean, while choosing not to attend college but rather Noah and their life together instead, has worked diligently encouraging Beverly, Brenda and "J. J." (John Jefferson) to obtain as much education as they wish. She has encouraged all three to be self-sufficient "Creekers."

Today, Nora Jean, is a loving grandmother and a "caring Creeker" who has a grace about her that aging cheerleaders do not often have; she is still "a star" at Carr Creek. (Courtesy of Sue Watts Miller)

Christine Reedy

Christine Reedy was born on Irishman Creek, the daughter of Hillis and Eliza Engle Reedy. Mr. Reedy, a well-known merchant, married a girl who lived in the orphanage and attended elementary and high school at Carr Creek Community Center.

Christine attended elementary and high school at Carr Creek riding the bus, five miles each way, from her Irishman Creek home. She was a student who had a tenacity—a penchant, if you please—for the highest academic grade possible. She worked diligently in every aspect of her life.

Christine met the criteria of a good, intelligent, beautiful Carr Creek cheerleader, and in her senior year the "voters" (students) secured a spot on the cheerleading squad for scholar Christine.

Christine graduated with honor from Carr Creek High School at age 16, in May 1956. She was the salutatorian of the class. In the fall of 1956, Christine Reedy (Godsey) enrolled at Berea College, Berea, Kentucky, graduating in 1960 with a Bachelor of Arts in English and Classical Literature.

After college, Christine married a young teacher, Maurice Godsey, from Happy (Perry County), Kentucky. They met at a church picnic. Christine and Maurice began a life of teaching, obtaining Masters of Education degrees at Miami University, Oxford, Ohio, and raising their family, Amy Lenore and Mark. Maurice taught at Princeton High School, but Christine chose to stay home for ten years after the children came, teaching, nurturing, and providing a home full of love and a strong educational environment.

When the children were securely on their developmental way, she began to teach at Fairfield High School, Fairfield, Ohio, for the next 28 years, retiring a few years ago. During her very productive years at Fairfield High School, she taught literature and classical languages, and at one point, she taught Latin for a few years. She was the advance placement instructor for a long period before retirement.

Today, Christine is an avid reader, belonging to a book club (or two) in the area, and also encouraging Maurice (member of the Fairfield School Board) in his school board work. They are strong advocates of education. Christine continues to keep a "scholarly hand" on her enjoyment and promotion of education as a consultant for Educational Testing Services, College Board, Princeton, New Jersey. She is an evaluator of essays and other written material by high school seniors for college credit. Thus, the educational environment provided in the home of this "Creeker" is so evident in the lives of Amy Lenore and Mark.

Amy Lenore (Alexander) graduated from Fairfield High School, Fairfield, Ohio, with the desire to teach. She later graduated from Hanover College, Hanover, Indiana, with a Bachelor of Arts in Education. She met and married another teacher, Andrew Alexander, from Scotland, and they lived and taught school there for three years before returning to Ohio to teach and be near Christine and Maurice. In January 2000, Amy and Andrew became the parents of "first grandson" Andrew Steven.

Mark graduated from Fairfield High School and Northwestern University, Evanston, Illinois, as a pre-law major. He was accepted at Ohio State University law school, holding the position of "number one" in his class all three years. Mark was a Federal Prosecutor as the Assistant United States Attorney for Attorney General Janet Reno in the United States Government Office in New York City. He is married to Kristin, the Features Editor of *Good Housekeeping* magazine. They are the parents of daughter Dana. (Sue Watts Miller)

I was asked to profile the cheerleaders and some of the basketball team. It has not been an easy task, even for a former Carr Creek cheerleader with "polished political skills." "The electorate" of the Carr Creek Elementary and High School "elected" me in 1948 and again, in 1949-50, to cheer for "our beloved Indians."

Never Forgotten: the Legacy of the 1956 Championship Cheerleaders

In 1956, all of the emphasis was on the basketball players and coaches. Occasionally, one or both team managers appeared in the write-ups by reporters covering the team for their particular newspaper. But very little was ever written about the cheerleaders. They were often thought of as an addendum or an appendage to the team.

It has been an interesting and enjoyable look into the lives of five women who were elected to cheer for Carr Creek High School's only championship team! All five beautiful, intelligent, and innately good women have taken their own paths to fulfillment.

It is interesting to note that while all Carr Creek cheerleaders found their "place in the sun" on Carr Creek Hill, they were not all as lucky as these five were to have the opportunity to cheer for such an outstanding group of young men. It was a rare combination of strong character athletic ability and inmate intelligence that both ball players and cheerleaders possessed as that entire squad found their own path to success in life. It seemed to be a very special group of young men and women intent on excelling in basketball, cheerleading, education, and their personal lives. They faced adversity in life as they cheered for or played basketball with tenacity and a faith in God. When *The Carr Creek Legacy* was published in 1995, it stirred a new interest in the 1956 Championship Team. Questions were asked at each book signing about the 1956 team: Where are they now? What are they doing? Whatever happened to those five cheerleaders?

We have shown with sincere joy and pride what became of the 1956 Carr Creek cheerleaders, as well as, those outstanding young men of championship caliber.

Once in a lifetime one is involved from "legacy and heart," with an outstanding group of individuals that found a way to succeed in life and in something called basketball.

This chapter on the 1956 cheerleaders of Carr Creek has been compiled and written by Sue Watts Miller, with much appreciated brief profiles from Peggy Lynn Collins (Hopper) and Polly Geraldine Mullins (Merritt).

9

"The Big Dipper"

He is called "the Big Dipper" in Hazard. Very few people know his real name. He has a sports radio call-in program with a large audience because he loves sports. On April 3, 1996, his program was called "The Carr Creek Story." Representing Carr Creek sports were Morton Combs, head coach of the Carr Creek team that won the 1956 state crown in Lexington, and Willard "Sprout" Johnson, who coached the 1948 Carr Creek team that won third place in the state. I was the other invitee (I felt truly honored to be a participant in this radio program). Ernest J. Sparkman, owner of radio station WGS, is the one who organized the format of this program. Mr. Sparkman graduated from Carr Creek in 1944 and has supported Carr Creek in every way down through the years. He was All-State in 1948. Several people were in the audience, including the governor's daughter. The following is exactly the way it transpired.

Dipper: Tonight we shall talk with Don Miller about his new book, *The Carr Creek Legacy*.

Dipper: Good evening, sports fans. We are live from the LaCitadel high on the mountain side overlooking Hazard and the surrounding mountains. Tonight is the final broadcast for the year and what a finale it will be. It is nice to see so many of you who wanted to be here in person. We welcome the daughter of Governor Patton with several friends in her group. Don received a big hug from his first cousin, Renee Stidom, the wife of Fred Stidom, superintendent of Hazard Independent Schools, and several others were there. This is going to be an exciting night for all of us. We have Don Miller, the author of *The Carr Creek Legacy* and a former all-stater who played for one of our guests, "Sprout" Johnson, and we have Morton Combs, whose 1956 Carr Creek team won the state basketball championships; we have Ernest J. Sparkman, the owner of WGS here in Hazard. He and his son, Shane, make it possible for us to have this program tonight. Remember, sports fans, you may call in and ask a question for any of our guests. This has been a great year for sports in Kentucky. Breathitt County won the state in football and Paintsville won the state championship in basketball.

Dipper: Don, tell us why you decided to write a book on the Carr Creek Legacy.

Miller: I have been wanting to do this for ten years. I have been teaching at Morehead State University for 29 years, and that kept me too busy to write a book. However, I had gathered most of the data when I retired, and this enabled me to spend most of my time putting the research together, and it gave me a quick start in the writing of this book. My wife and I worked very hard to get this research into book form. It really is difficult to write a book—but I'm glad that I did, because we learned so much about our school that we did not know existed. I wrote the book because it is about the only way to preserve the history of any school that has been consolidated.

Dipper: Don, I know that in 1948, Carr Creek made a very good showing. Who did you lose to?

Miller: Well, we lost to Maysville by three points in an overtime in the semifinal. We had the ball and leading Maysville by three points; I was trying to run out the clock by dribbling from one place to another, and a foul was called on *me*. That was the fifth foul and I had to take a seat on the bench. I did not feel too badly, because we were up three points with only 35 seconds to go. There was a new rule that had just been voted in during the 1947-48 basketball season and it probably cost us the game. You had the choice of shooting or taking the ball out of bounds on the side. (The bonus free throw—if you made the first you got another shot—was not in the rule book.) Maysville took the ball out on the side and threw it to Maysville's center, and he turned around and made the basket and was fouled on the shot—

he made the foul shot and tied the game. With our starting center out and I was out and we had little depth, so they beat us 56–54 in overtime.

Dipper: Every basketball fan has heard of the 1928 team and what it accomplished in 1928. I had heard about this team myself, and *The Carr Creek Legacy* made it clear what transpired that season. A member of that squad was Willard Johnson. Mr. Johnson, I understand that only one is still living?

Johnson: At the present time only one of the starting five is still living. The player is Mr. Gurney Adams and he lives with his daughter in Nicholasville, Kentucky. (Mr. Adams, the last of the 1928 Carr Creek team, passed away in 1998.) Another player on the squad, Mr. Carson Cornette, lives in Louisville.

Dipper: Sprout, your whole life has been associated with Carr Creek.

Johnson: Well, I might have to brag a little. I was born and raised at Carr Creek. The only time that I was away from Carr Creek was when I attended Morehead Teacher's College for four years. I have had the honor of being involved with the five Carr Creek teams that went to the state tournament. I was a substitute on the 1928 team, I started on the 1930 and 1931 state teams. I was the coach of the 1948 team that finished third in the state, and I was an assistant coach on the 1956 team that won the state championship. In five games in the state our record was 11 wins and four losses. For the national tournament Carr Creek was 3-1.

Dipper: I noticed that in 1930-31, that Carr Creek and Hazard were in the state tournament. How could that happen?

Johnson: Well, we had an "A" class and a "B" class. Hazard, being one of the bigger schools, and they played in each tournament as an "A" team. Carr Creek, being a much smaller school, played all "B" teams in each tournament. Each of us played in our class at the regional level. Carr Creek won the regional "B" tournament, but Hazard lost its "A" game for the regional crown. It was the same for our 1928 team. What this does is to guarantee that there shall be eight small teams and eight large teams making up the "Sweet Sixteen." To get to the final game of the state, Carr Creek defeated three "B" teams. In the first game, Carr Creek won over Walton High School 31–11; in the quarter finals, Carr Creek defeated Minerva, 21–11, in the semifinals Carr Creek defeated Lawrenceburg 37–11 in a big upset because Lawrenceburg was selected by many sportswriters and fans to win it all. Carr Creek was the winner in the class "B" title. Ashland won the class "A" title by beating Danville, Henderson, and Covington for the class "A" crown. The tournament was not over. Now these two schools played for the championship of the state. How much better was class "A" Ashland than class "B" champion? Well, not much, as Ashland did win 13–11 in four overtimes! For their good showing in the state tournament, Carr Creek along with Ashland were invited to the National Basketball High School Tournament at the University of Chicago. We did well and won three games against the best competition from each state. In fact, we beat Austin (Texas) High School, which was the favorite of the tournament. Ashland won it all. Was Carr Creek as good as most teams in the nation? No one else played Ashland to four overtime periods!

Dipper: Morton, your life was mostly spent at Carr Creek as a coach and principal.

Morton: That's right.

Dipper: You went to high school at Hazard and won it all in 1932. You only scored one field goal but it was enough to beat Louisville Male by 15–13.

Morton: I thought that I could never top the thrill of making the winning goal. However, I have to be honest, winning the state championship with the 1956 Carr Creek team was my biggest thrill in basketball.

Dipper: I have been asked for you to tell the fans how long was that shot you made against Louisville Male. Some say it was a lay-up and others said you were closer than that. (A good deal of laughter followed that comment.)

Morton: I know you won't believe it, but it would have been a three-shot range of today. A two-hand shot because the one-hand shot was seldom used in 1932.

Dipper: The shooting of a basketball has changed so much in the last ten years or so. And it is known that Carr Creek has always had good shooters.

Morton: We have been very fortunate to have great shooters, and Don Miller sitting across from me was one of these great shooters, but what made him so valuable was his hustle, and he was very intelligent on the court and in the classroom. I think that one big reason that our players shot well was because they played all through the summer on outdoor basketball courts. And they loved the game. And we have another former Carr Creek great, Ernest Sparkman. For most of the years that Ernest J. played at Carr Creek, he was like a man playing with boys. Ernest, I think, was the tallest boy to ever play at Carr Creek. He was a little over 6'6" tall. He was quick in his moves because he was not heavy, and he was not awkward for his size.

Dipper: Go ahead, you are on the air.

Paul: I congratulate you on your selection of these three guests. They all have outstanding knowledge of the game of basketball. I have a question for the guests. What do you think about the three-point line, and other changes in basketball rules down through the years that you fellows played and coached? Have the changes made basketball more exciting than it is today?

Morton: I did not like the rule where you could either shoot the foul shot, or take the ball out of bounds. I feel that you should have to shoot the foul shots. I really like the three-pointer; in fact, I suggested that a long time ago. I also suggested raising the goal six inches higher.

Paul: Do you like the rule where it is alternate possessions when two players tie up?

Morton: Yes, I can go along with that. I feel that high school basketball should be speeded up.

Dipper: Okay, we have another caller on the line. (Ver-

non Cooper, caller.) Go ahead and ask your question or questions to our panel.

Cooper: I remember the 1928 Carr Creek team and I read Don Miller's book on this team, and I still don't see how these young men succeeded against all odds. Sprout, could you talk about this team?

Johnson: In 1928 there was a national high school basketball tournament on the campus of the University of Chicago. Usually only one school from each state is invited to this tournament. Carr Creek and Ashland were invited. Carr Creek was chosen primarily for their showing against Ashland in the state tournament. This was the 10th annual tournament. In 1931, the tournament ended because of the major depression in the United States. It was never revived. To my knowledge, we were the only small team from Kentucky to play in this tournament. Only two other high schools in Kentucky played in the national tournament. The others were Lexington High School (now Henry Clay). Ashland that won the nationals in 1928.

After we had beaten Bristol, Connecticut, the school presented each player a watch that read *Congratulations from Bristol High School.* That one act of kindness from a school we had beaten made a big impression on all of us.

Dipper: You are on the air.

Powell: Hello to you and your guests. I am coach James Powell of Powell County. I tell you, Dip, I am really enjoying this, and I wanted to call and let you and your guests know how proud I am of your guests, who are winners. Good guys don't always finish last. These people are proof of that.

Dipper: I follow your girl's team and I know you are disappointed that your star, Heather Baker, was not selected to try out for the girl's All Star's Team.

Powell: Well, you are correct. The *Lexington Herald-Leader* has her on the first team for the All-State list. She averaged over 30 points a game. Heather took it all in good stride, which doesn't surprise me. She knew what she wanted when the University of Louisville came through with a basketball scholarship.

Dipper: Don, you are a credit to all mountain basketball fans—just wait a second, Don, we have another caller. *(David Adams, caller.)*

David: Who leads the scoring average for the Carr Creek Indians? I know that might be a tough question because I'm not sure the records were kept in the earlier days. Second, what team holds the record for winning the most games in a row before a loss?

Dipper: Mr. Johnson, I shall direct this question to you on who was the all-time leading scorer for Carr Creek.

Johnson: David has stumped me on that question because I have had so many players who scored high for me. Morton, do you know or have any idea who scored the most points?

Morton: No, I don't have any idea, but in my first year (1938) at Carr Creek, we won 23 games and lost just once. But I can't remember how many we won in a row.

Miller: As far as the all-time scorer is concerned, I would think it would have been someone in the last decade, because of the rules changes. The game is much faster today and scores in the 90s were not uncommon in the last 10 to 15 years. In 1948, when Carr Creek was third in the state tournament, my cousin (Bill Morton) and I tied for the most points scored (57) that was just under 15 points for four games.

Dipper: Sprout, when did you and Morton meet?

Johnson: Of course, I followed the 1932 team when he was playing in the season and state tournament. I'm positive we crossed paths that year. At this time he was a Hazard boy who we wanted to beat. Then when he came to Carr Creek as teacher and coach, he met with immediate success. I used to be able to name these boys who played under Morton from 1938-41, but they were very strong and talented. Don, in your research for your book, I'm sure you could name some of these players.

Miller: It is during this time that my dad would take me to their games. Gail Amburgey, Ellis Adams, Vadis Bach, and others came from Breeding's Creek. Here are my favorites during the three years Morton coached: Bach and Amburgey, Adams, George Armstrong, and Ernest J. Sparkman.

Dipper: Don, I want you to tell the fans here in Hazard where they may buy a book. There are a few books in the shopping center where Cliff Hagan's Restaurant is located. Right now I can't recall the name of the store. Quillen's store in Whitesburg, the Hindman library, the mini-mall (Holly

Hills in Hindman), Joseph Beth bookstore in Lexington (they have sold out four times). If anyone can't find one, then give me a call, and I shall see that you get a book.

I also would like to comment on Morton and Sprout. These two men have touched the lives of many Carr Creekers who were in their classes and on the basketball court. They directed us toward a bigger goal—the preparation for life. Scores of us received a basketball scholarship to several colleges. They encouraged us to set high goals, then work hard to achieve this mindset to allow yourself to succeed. That was the goal of the 1956 state champs—to be winners—and they succeeded.

These two men coached their teams without running up and down the sidelines ranting and raving at the officials and players. In the seven years that I played for Sprout, I never heard one vulgar word from him, and he never chewed out any player that could be embarrassing for the player.

Morton has this same class. I have watched Morton coach in several games, and he was always in control. Morton told me something interesting about Carr Creek: "With all our success, we never had one regional or district tournament on our floor. We always had to play in someone else's gym."

Dipper: Ernest (Sparkman), you have played for both Morton and Sprout. What are your comments about these two gentlemen?

Ernest: Well, it was a great experience being coached by both. During 1938-41 Morton had great players and won most of his games. When Morton left for the army in 1941, then I was coached by Sprout. Sprout coached until his retirement from coaching after the 1953-54 season. Morton then returned as principal and coach. Today, I just think of them as close friends. I now look at these gentlemen as good teachers, always willing to help a student as they would in helping an athlete. They are a lot more than just being a coach. Each has a fine family. They are active in church where they help in anything they are asked to serve Our Lord. Each has definitely been a role model for the students and to others. I feel that basketball is just a small part in the lives of these two gentlemen.

Dipper: I'm looking at a 1944 Carr Creek picture that has the cheerleaders in it. The caption under this picture show two cheerleaders, Irene Combs and Dulcie Amburgey, having their arms around your neck. Does this mean that you were a ladies' man in high school *(laughter)*?

Ernest: Oh, no, no, I was just—no, that isn't so.

(It was the first time that Ernest really was caught off guard. His struggling to get back on track was not going to be easy. Everyone in the room just broke out in laughter. Finally, he sarcastically said he was not liked by the girls. Another chuckle from the crowd.)

Dipper: In 1944, Ernest, Carr Creek beat Harlan on the Vicco High floor. Their star player was Wallace "Wah Wah" Jones. Jones was around 6'5" and weighed about 230 pounds. Jones had scored 82 points against a Harlan County team two nights before our game.

Ernest: The team got together with Sprout and we decided no one was going to score that many against us. We were really up for this game. We beat them 47–37. I am very proud of this victory. As I remember, Jones and I scored 18 points each. The Harlan team went on to win the Kentucky High School State Tournament. We lost in the finals of the 14th Regional. Here is a good example of a fine Carr Creek team not making it to the state tournament. As Morton stated before, the 1956 Carr Creek State Champion probably was not as good as the 1955 team and his 1963 team. Morton has mentioned two things you must have if you win the state championship: a good team that plays together, and you have to be lucky. He had these ingredients with his 1956 team. It was just sad that we didn't make it to the state.

Dipper: Of course, Jones went on to the University of Kentucky and was an All-American in basketball and also a fine baseball and football player for the Wildcats. Ernest also went to U of K on a basketball scholarship in 1945, and after one year, you went into the Army Air Corps.

Ernest: I guess one little incident that occurred in Madison Square Garden between Rupp and I shall be the only thing that people shall remember me by, is this happening, but I did do a lot more than that. In fact, I helped them win some games my freshman year as a backup center to Alex Groza. I have many happy memories at the University of Kentucky. After my time in the Air Corps, I did not go back to the University of Kentucky; instead, I went to Minneapolis to study broadcasting.

Dipper: I have one more question for you, Ernest. What kind of influence did Morton and Sprout have on your life?

Ernest: A great impact, as most youngsters have who played for these two men or sat under them in class. These two men have had the biggest influence on my life, and Don Miller shall attest to that.

I have one last question to ask of Morton and Sprout. Morton, I shall go to you first. You went to Hazard and your team won the state championship when you scored the winning basket over Louisville Male 15–13. You won the state championship with Carr Creek in 1956. What is your highlight?

Morton: Of course, there were many highlights. Certainly playing on Hazard's state championship team and to shoot the winning shot was the highlight at that time. But to be honest, there is nothing like taking your own team, working and coaching them for days and days throughout approximately six months, and then see them win our final goal—the state championship. This has to be the highlight of my basketball career. However, another great highlight was taking my 1963 team to Louisville to play in the Louisville Invitational Tournament, by far the most prestigious tournament, and most of these teams were favored to win their regions. When we arrived at Louisville, it was the coldest day on record at that time. Our bus driver, Sid Adams, did a wonderful job driving over many frozen spots on the road. We were happy to be at our hotel.

We won the first two games over Louisville teams, and we had to play Elizabethtown in the semifinal game, and they were favored over us. We won that game and faced Louisville Seneca for the final. Seneca was rated the number-one team in the state. Their two best players were Mike Redd and Wesley Unseld. They had not lost a game. We played a great game and won the championship. However, it was a bittersweet victory for us. Our best player, Lewis Couch, who sustained a badly sprained ankle and did not get to play in the district tournament, and we lost to Hindman in the district. If you recall, I made the statement that for a team to win the state tournament, it had to be good (which we were) and also be lucky (we weren't). We were the only team to beat Seneca as they went on to capture the state tournament again. Winning this Louisville Invitational was also a great thrill.

I have loved basketball, as a player and as a coach, and I knew in high school and also when I was in college that I was going to be a basketball coach. If I could have afforded it, I would have coached for nothing. I almost did. In 1938, while coaching Carr Creek, my salary was about 20 dollars a month.

Danny Hall *(caller):* I'm a graduate of Carr Creek; though I didn't play basketball, I followed the 1963 team at home and away. I was not at the L.I.T. games because of the bad weather. I listened to the final game in my dad's house. When we won I was so excited that I stood up and threw my right fist and hand into the air, and my fist went through the ceiling. I was in classes with Glen (Morton's son), and I truly enjoyed my years at Carr Creek.

Dipper: Thanks for calling. Morton, tell us something about your best teams.

Morton: Well, in 1955, there were three teams good enough to win the state. It was Hazard in the 34th District, and Hindman and Carr Creek in the 55th District. Each team had won and lost to each other during the season. Every game had gone down to the wire. Each was highly rated in the state. In the Regional draw, all three teams drew in the same bracket. Hazard won the war and then went on to be state champs. Goebel Ritter of Hazard made the remark that Hindman and Carr Creek would have won the state. Incidentally, Carr Creek lost to Hazard in the final game of the regional in—you guessed it—in an overtime period. As previously stated, Carr Creek never had the district or regional at Carr Creek gym, and that is a big disadvantage to us. Also, we had the smallest enrollment of most of the schools we played. I do want to say this about tiny Cordia High, definitely one of the smallest schools in the Commonwealth. The year we won the tournament in 1956, we just beat Cordia by one in the Hazard Invitational Tournament. They never beat us, but for some reason, Cordia always played us tough. I had tremendous respect for their coach, George Cornette, and I always hoped that his team could make it to the state tournament. There were times that they could have gone with just a little luck. I know that Don remembers the state team he played on in 1948, that Cordia played them to the wire in the district that year. Carr Creek went on to win by a large margin in the three games of the regional at Hazard.

Dipper: We shall break a few minutes and come right back with our guests, Don Miller, Sprout Johnson, Morton Combs, and Ernest J. Sparkman.

You are on the air.

Don Johnson (caller): I'm calling from Plant City, Florida. Just wanted to call and tell Mr. Combs and Mr. Johnson how great it was to have had the opportunity to play basketball for them.

Dipper: Don Johnson, when did you play for these two gentlemen?

Don Johnson: I played from 1967-69. I had a brother who played on the 1963 team that was the L.I.T. His name was Bobby Ray Johnson.

Morton: There was another relative you had who played for me—your father.

Don Johnson: That's right. If my dad is listening to this show, he is going to cut me out of his will (lots of laughter).

Caller: I have a question for Mr. Combs (the caller also is from Florida).

Dipper: All right, go ahead.

Caller: I understand that he caught a 16-pound bass down here, and I would like to know where he caught it. (Lots of laughter.)

Morton: I caught it in Florida right in the tough part of the mouth (more laughter). I caught it in the Florida straits.

Ernest J: You cannot believe what Morton says about that fish. I saw it, and every time Morton tells it, the fish gets longer and the weight is increased. But it was a nice one. The *Tampa Tribune* did have a story about it.

Dipper: Don, thank you very much for your call.

Caller, Jane Calhoun Couch: Hello, this is Jane Calhoun Couch. It is so nice to hear from you tonight. It's been a long time since that state championship in 1956.

Morton: Yes, it has, but there's hardly been a day that goes by that I don't remember all of you.

Dipper: If my memory serves me correctly, you are related to Jim Calhoun.

Jane: I'm his older, wiser sister.

Dipper: I know that you are proud of Jim, but also, his outstanding four years at the University of Cincinnati, where he played on two national championships and a teammate was Oscar Robinson.

Jane: Yes, that is correct, and I married E. A. Couch and have two sons: Joey Couch, who played football and graduated from the University of Kentucky. David is a graduate of West Point.

Dipper: I shall have to tell you that Joey told a golfing story on me but I shall let it go this time. However, he is a character.

Miller: Jane, my name is Don Miller, and your son Joey's supervisor is my son, Terry Michael Miller, and Terry loves him. Joey has won about all the awards that a sales representative can win. We now consider Joey as a member of our family. He is a wonderful young man. I am looking forward to meeting your son David. One son a graduate of the University of Kentucky and another a graduate of West Point—you and E. A. have to be wonderful parents, and that thrills me very much. (David played for Krzyzewski at Army.)

Jane: We moved back to Paintsville because we wanted them under some great teachers who cared about the students. We have never been sorry. Of course, we loved our time at Carr Creek when I was a cheerleader and E. A. a basketball player under two of the greatest in Mr. Combs and Mr. Johnson.

Morton: Jane, Don and I were talking about you and E. A. just a few days ago, because we would like to get together with you.

Jane: We need to get that 1956 team together. We need to work on that. It would be a great time for all of us.

Morton: I agree.

Johnson: One last thing that I wanted to get across tonight was Carr Creek's relationship with Ashland High. Of course, in 1928 we played Ashland and lost 13–11 in four overtime periods. During the season of 1944-45, Ashland built a new gymnasium, so Carr Creek was invited to christen the new facility. Don was a freshman at that time and he worked himself into a starting position. Don's brother, Sherrill, was a senior and our center. Paul McGraner, Farmer Couch, and Ellis Amburgey rounded out the first five. We won the game—in an overtime! John McGill of Ashland (a sportswriter) had a nice article about the game and the other one (1928).

Dipper: Morton, talk about your son, Glen; he was a great player in high school and he was an all-American at Virginia Tech and then played as a professional for several years.

Morton: Glen did have a good high school career. However, he was young and not really that strong. It was in college during his sophomore season that he started to blossom. He gained some weight and strength and reached 6'2" in height, and he was on his way for a great career in basketball; played in the ABC and with the Utah Jazz in the National Basketball Association. He lives in Roanoke, Virginia, now. His wife is from there. He has been very successful as a businessman.

Dipper: Hello, you are on the air.

Caller: Big Dipper, this is Joey Couch. I'm calling from Paintsville.

Dipper: Joey Couch! Ha! Ha! Ha!. I'm not going to have you back at our banquet because of that golf story you told on me. Ha! Ha!

Joey, you can't believe how good it is to hear from you. I have talked with people this week who were from Paintsville and they had great things to say about you and the Paintsville teams you played on. (Joey played on the 1985, 1986, and 1987 basketball teams that went to the state all three years.)

Joey: This is a dream come true for me. I never had the

chance to talk with Mr. Combs and Mr. Johnson; but I feel that you are members of our family because of the high praise and respect my dad and mom have for you two gentlemen. I think the values instilled in me from mom and dad go back to you men. That one has to work hard and sacrifice things to be a winner, and I know that was true for the Carr Creek team that won the 1956 state tournament, and it was true for us who played on the successful Paintsville teams of the past. When my Uncle Jim Calhoun and my dad would get together and most of their conversation was about that 1956 team and I would listen intently on everything that was said, and how I wished something like that could be a part of my life. And it almost happened. I was on three state tournaments for Paintsville, and was selected on the all-tournament and All-State teams.

Dipper: Joey, I have this picture of the 1956 team in my office, and the little "chubby" fellow in the middle is me. As you know, the team stopped in Hazard on their way home where the team members and coaches were honored. People were taking pictures and I had to be in one. I truly treasure this picture and to be in it with your dad, E. A., and your uncle, Jim Calhoun, is a special honor.

Joey: When I read Mr. Miller's book, *The Carr Creek Legacy*, I could not believe how long ago this tradition of excellence in basketball and academic excellence continued at this small school.

(Sue and I showed the slides that are more than 75 years old about the building of the early classrooms at Carr

Creek to a district meeting with my son, Terry Michael. I approached Joey and I told him if the players, cheerleaders, and coaches of the 1956 team would give me their approval, I would write a book about them. I wasn't ready for Joey's response—he gave me a big hug and said, "My dad and mother would love it and I would too." I hope you like it, Joey. Your Uncle Jim Calhoun has helped me immensely with gathering research for me.)

Joey: I am talking to you from the highest peak that I could find in Johnson County. My mother informed me about the broadcast and I just was compelled to call. I don't know all of you personally, but I am not ashamed to say that I love all of you, and Mr. Miller, your son Terry is a tremendous person. He is really fun to work for.

Dipper: Don't leave us, Joey; Morton wants to say something.

Morton: I try not to single anyone out, but I have to tell you about this Couch family. I had all those boys and they all were outstanding players and wonderful people. Jim, Jane's brother and now E. A.'s brother-in-law—and I count him as in the Couch family—was an outstanding player, and Jane was a cheerleader and always kept things going in the right direction. Carr Creek High has always been like a family. Many of these families, like the Couch family, made Carr Creek what it accomplished down through the years.

Dipper: I can't believe we are out of time. What a way to end this season's finale. Thank you, Don Miller. I now see why so many people hold you in high esteem. Your book has to be made into a movie. I thank you, Sprout and Morton, for your warm and sincere descriptions concerning players, cheerleaders, and everyone else you two gentlemen had contact with. Of course, this really is an Ernest J. Sparkman production. His son, Shane, is grinning because he knows who did all the manual labor.

Dipper: I shall be with you again in the fall. Have a great summer.

10
The Carr Creek Influence

A Converted Creeker, by Howard McCann

Small schools in Kentucky have always intrigued me. Growing up in Lewis County, Kentucky, in the 1950s and early 1960s, I attended Heselton, a two-room school in Big Salt Lick in rural Lewis County. The old school is now caving in, but I have so many fond memories of my friends and family during our youth. The Heselton school was very much a part of our little community and has had a lifetime effect on me. My wife Barbara, daughter Sarah, and I have traveled extensively in the state of Kentucky seeking out small schools, and this fascination led us to our latest adventure. My adventure initially began when I was a freshman at Lewis County High School in Vanceburg, Kentucky, in 1964. Our coach, Ray Allen, was from McDowell, Kentucky. Coach Allen decided to take our baseball team on a mountain trip. We played teams from McDowell, Martin, Maytown, Wheelwright, Virgie, Wayland, and Dorton. After that trip I tried to follow the mountain schools and their sports teams. I have tried to read everything available and finally struck gold.

A couple of years ago, while discussing Kentucky high school basketball with two of my old Kentucky buddies in Dayton, Ohio, Herald Ratliff and Larry Bates, I was informed of a new book about the legendary Carr Creek High School entitled *The Carr Creek Legacy* by Don Miller. After looking over the book, I asked Herald where I could get one. Herald responded that Don Miller was an old friend of his and that he would write to Don to see if he had any books left. Around two weeks passed and I received a call from Herald asking me to come over and discuss Kentucky high school basketball. When I arrived, to my surprise, Herald handed me my autographed copy of *The Carr Creek Legacy*. This book touched me in numerous ways, and I sat down and finished it in its entirety. I called Don to thank him for his wonderful book. I enjoyed listening to his stories about Carr Creek High School, the people in the community, and especially the coaches. I was inspired to take another trip to see Carr Creek and other schools including Hindman, Inez, Hazard, McDowell, Virgie, and Garrett. Our first stop would be the old Carr Creek High School.

It was a great stop. A resident who lives close to the school saw us taking pictures, and after he saw our interest, he opened the door to the gym and let us in. His name is David Adams. I took pictures and videoed some on the inside. It pleases me to see an old school and gym still in good shape (so many I visited were in such bad shape and beyond repair). Don told me that his senior year was when the gym was completed, and they almost won the state in 1948. I thought of the 1956 team and the great players on that team that won the state championship. It was difficult to believe that such a small school on a hillside could win it all.

David showed us where Coach Morton Combs lived. I would have loved to have talked with him, but David said he wasn't home at this time.

David showed us where Mr. Willard Johnson lived. The Johnsons were home, and when I said Don Miller's name, both he and his wife smiled. (I had it made after that.) We had a great time visiting with them. I had *The Legacy* with me, and as we left, we had each one to autograph the book, too.

(This probably was the last signature for Sprout. Four days later he had a stroke and never recovered. Howard also took a picture of Nelle and Sprout on their front porch. It really was a good picture of them. I cannot thank Howard enough for what he did.)

I could not believe how beautiful it was on the Carr Creek campus. I tried to visualize what it must have been like in 1956 when Carr Creek and Wayland high schools came down from the hills to see who would be crowned "King of the Mountains." I thought of what it must have been like sitting in the Carr Creek gym watching Coach Combs and his assistant, Mr. Johnson, coaching the 1956 basketball team. I would have loved to have had the opportunity to be there when Carr Creek brought the state championship trophy home. They were truly "Kings of the Mountains."

11
The Good Samaritans

This story has a direct connection with the 1956 Carr Creek State Champions, especially E. A. Couch and Freddie Maggard. This article refers to Joey Couch, son of E. A., and Freddie Maggard, Jr., son of Freddie Maggard of the 1956 team. E. A. and Freddie are great buddies, but each traveled a different road after graduation. Freddie settled in Cumberland, Kentucky, and E. A., after playing for the University of Kentucky and University of Dayton, lived a few years in Ohio, but moved his family to Paintsville so that his two sons could start school in Kentucky.

Joey was a fine basketball and football star at Paintsville High. Meanwhile, Freddie Jr. was a fine basketball and football star at Cumberland. Every Kentucky high school sports fan thought both of these outstanding young men would attend a college and play basketball—just look at what their dads accomplished in winning the state championship in 1956. Who would have thought that the two would come to the University of Kentucky on *football* scholarships? Freddie Jr. played quarterback and Joey was a noseguard. Of course, the two bonded quickly and were roommates at UK for five years.

They sometimes speak of Jerry Bell in the past tense, of how he was, how much fun he was to be around, and some of the outrageous things he would do. Freddie and Joey speak as if he is gone, for in a tangible way, the Jerry Bell they knew is gone—but in a sense, he is not gone completely.

It's the Jerry Bell who is still here, somehow miraculously here on this earth, still living, still breathing, still making strides, whom Joey Couch and Freddie Maggard, Jr., want to help.

"I know that if this had happened to me," Maggard said, "Jerry would be doing the same things for me."

Freddie and Joey don't want this close friend forgotten.

Freddie Maggard last played with Jerry Bell in 1991, but he's never stopped being his teammate.

That's why Maggard, a former University of Kentucky quarterback, still regularly visits Bell, a former University of Kentucky defensive tackle, even though it breaks his heart. Bell will never be the same character Maggard loved from their very first meeting—when Bell brandished a frog-gigging spear at his new summer roommate and said, "Touch any of my stuff, I'll kill you. Want to go to McDonald's?"

It happened on a Friday, Good Friday to be exact, in 1997. What happened is not exactly known. The only one who knows for sure, Bell himself, cannot talk other than to say hi and his name. It has only been recently that he has started to walk again.

Whatever the circumstances, a gun was fired, and a .357 magnum bullet ripped into the right side of the head of the former defensive tackle of the University of Kentucky, leaving him for dead.

Only he didn't die. Bell emerged from a coma three months later, but his life never would be the same.

"I don't know of any school that has gone through the things that Kentucky has gone through with its former players," Maggard said. "We need to do something to get together and help each other out. We need more of that."

Start with Ted Presly, a walk-on defensive back who died of a gunshot wound while apparently playing Russian roulette in April 1992.

Go to Trent DiGurio, who was murdered while sitting on his front porch after a party at the house he and some teammates were renting in July 1994. The murder is still unsolved. Then a few Novembers ago—a truck accident involving Jason Watts, teammate Artie Steinmetz, and Scott Brock.

Then recently a former offensive guard, Jeremy Streck, while crossing a street at 3:00 a.m., was run down by a car, its driver allegedly under the influence. A week later, Streck died. "It's just unbelievable to me," Maggard said.

"Jerry Bell was a nut. His friends would be the first to tell you that. He was one of those wild and crazy, do-almost-anything kind of guy who could crack you up in a second. There was never a dull moment around Jerry," Couch said.

He was also a good football player, 6'4", 280-pound defensive tackle from Louisville DeSales High who lettered from 1988-91, playing for Jerry Claiborne and then for Bill Curry. On the field, Bell was nagged by injuries. He was named to the Football News All-American Freshman Team in 1988.

Off the field, the trio were great friends. The two eastern Kentucky boys bonded with the wild man from Louisville.

"He, Joey, and I, we did everything together," says Maggard.

"The things we did, the conversations we had," Couch said, "I wish I could have bottled those things."

Playing against a Mississippi team, Bell told Joey and Freddie that since the game was being televised, that he was going to get TV exposure by faking to be hurt on a play so the TV cameras would zoom in for a close shot. In the first half, Bell fell down with a sprained ankle. He stayed on the ground for a long time. Joey walked over to him and said, "Okay, Jerry, you can get up now. They've seen you on TV." Then Bell said, "No, no, I really am hurt." He was over on the sideline for the rest of the game—much to the amusement of Couch and Maggard.

"Jerry was crazy," Maggard said, "but you won't find anyone with a bigger heart than him."

"He was a kid at heart, but what a caring person he was," Couch said. "He'd do anything for you."

When they heard the news about the shooting that Easter weekend in 1997, Couch and Maggard both went to the hospital. "When I got there to see him, I can't explain how bad it was," Couch said. "It was one of the saddest things I've ever seen."

"I was still in the army in Orlando, Florida," Maggard said. "They were getting ready to send me to the desert. I got an emergency leave and came back. When Joey and I saw him, Joey just hit the floor."

When he got back to the army, Maggard was sure that Jerry was dead. The doctors didn't give much chance for him to live. "When I found out he was still alive, I couldn't believe it."

Maggard and Couch have kept in close contact, seeing or calling their old friend on a regular basis. "My work is demanding, but I try to talk to him once a month," Couch said, "and I think about him all the time."

Now, Bell lives with his parents, Jerry Lynn and Mary Bell, in Louisville. A friend from high school, Dawn Feltz, comes and helps out as much as she can. Jerry Lynn has had brain cancer and open-heart surgery. "You think, How many bad things can happen to one family?" Couch said.

"After what happened to Jerry," Maggard states, "I'm not some liberal activist, but I will never, ever own a handgun."

Now Freddie Wayne Maggard comes by more because his army term is up, and he now works for the Department of Military Affairs at a new school on the base at Fort Knox, which is not far from Louisville. He teaches at-risk youth and high school dropouts.

Freddie and Joey have a driven desire to help their good buddy in a financial bind. Before UK played LSU a few years ago, the two held a golf outing for Jerry at the Connemaria Golf Course outside Nicholasville. It was not as well attended as the two had hoped, but it was a start. They want to make it an annual event, the Friday of homecoming weekend, to help Bell and maybe others who need it. (I am an avid golfer and I did not know this event was taking place or I would have been there. It needs more media coverage.)

"UK does a lot of different things to help different people and help different causes, and that's great," Maggard said. "But I think we need to do more to try and get together and help each other. We all played at the University of Kentucky, and for the Commonwealth, and there are others I know that need help, and we need to get together and help everybody out. We should be doing that. That's the right thing to do."

"We just want to do what we can to help Jerry and his family," Couch said. "That's all we can do."

"To me," Maggard said, "that's what friends are for."

Why do these young men have a burden on their hearts to help a friend? It was the way they were raised. Helping others in need was a way of life for most families and friends of eastern Kentucky. It was instilled in their schools. E. A. Couch and his wife, Jane Calhoun, worked hard and supported Joey and his brother David. They knew the difference between right and wrong. Their ethical character and morals began at home, and these characteristics have never left Joey and Freddie Maggard, Jr.

I am proud that they are connected to the 1956 team.

(Some of this chapter is courtesy of the Lexington Herald-Leader.)

12
Time Does Change

The following was written by Mike Fields of the *Lexington Herald-Leader* in 1987 about the changing times since the 1956 Carr Creek team took the championship.

"Freddie Maggard, who lives in Cumberland, has come back to Carr Creek on a quiet Sunday afternoon to visit with his former coach, Morton Combs, and a couple of teammates, Jim Calhoun and John C. Mullins (1987). After watching a NCAA basketball game on television at Combs' house, the four men walk next door to the Carr Creek gym. It is dark and desolate. Maggard finds a basketball in a corner, steps onto the court, and fires up an awkward 22 footer. It misses badly. "It's been a long time," Maggard says with a laugh.

"It has been a long time, and in more ways than Freddie

Maggard meant. When tiny Carr Creek High School came out of Knott County to win the 1956 state championship, it was a different era. The mountain schools were kings of Kentucky high school basketball back then. Carr Creek was the third straight team from the coal fields to win the state title, following Inez in 1954 and Hazard in 1955.

"The day after Carr Creek won its championship, a headline in the *Lexington Herald-Leader* posed this question: 'Who is going to end the mountains' hold on the state title?'

"As Sweet Sixteen history tells us, Eastern Kentucky's reign came to an end after Carr Creek's victory. In 30 state tournaments since, no true mountain team has won the championship. In fact, only one representative—Clay County in 1985—has even reached the title game." (Paintsville won it all in 1996.)

Why the drought? The reasons are varied. They include integration, consolidation, and the automobile. The year after Carr Creek won the crown, black schools were allowed into the state tournament for the first time. Carr Creek High was the first high school to play an all-black school, Louisville Central, before integration was mandated.

In 1956, there were 520 boys' basketball teams in Kentucky; in 1987, there were 276 teams. It was called consolidation: more big schools overwhelm the small schools today. (This move took the heart out of small communities whose people were proud and extremely loyal to their small community schools. Control was much better. The students did not have to spend four hours on a bus to get them to the school and back. Today, educators are trying to downsize the schools for better discipline control.)

The automobile has also influenced the decrease in mountain teams' holding the title by decreasing the number of players. "Basketball used to be the only thing in the mountains," said Jim Calhoun. "It was your recreation and your respect. Today, the students have cars and do about whatever they want to do—not all these things are positive."

The 1956 Carr Creek team wasn't viewed as Cinderella in sneakers, however. In fact, the Indians entered the Sweet Sixteen as one of the favorites.

Carr Creek Coach Morton Combs and his right hand man, Assistant Coach Willard "Sprout" Johnson, had put together a team with a perfect blend of inside strength, outside shooting, teamwork, discipline, and depth. The starting five usually featured the 6'2" Couch. Bobby Ray Shepherd, a bullish 6'4"; 6'2" Warren Amburgey up front; and 6'2" Freddie Maggard and Calhoun, 5'10", in the back court. Ed Richardson, 5'10", also started in some games. All were seniors except Calhoun, who was a sophomore. Off the bench they relied on John C. Mullins, Marcus Combs, Ray Stamper, and Estill Adams.

13
Lest We Forget

I am including this article to help the reader feel the atmosphere of basketball and academics in the very beginning of the school. The following information was written by Ruth Weston and Olive Marsh. These two ladies come from upper New England. They were big workers in the D.A.R., and Alice Lloyd contacted them to help the Carr Creek school in getting started. The article was taken from *The Farmer's Wife*, September 1921, called UP ON SINGIN' CARR.

"Movie producers and novel writers have discovered that there is always a drawing interest in stories of the remote places of our great country where isolated communities live their lives and fought their battles for existence. But fiction or part fiction is never quite so full of interest as the real thing and this story of the mountain folks 'up on singin'

Carr' was written for *The Farmer's Wife* by special request of the editors.

We have a true story that brims over what is called technically "the humanities." Miss Marsh and Miss Weston were very educated and graduates of prestigious Northeastern colleges. They made great sacrifices to lead to these mountain seekers after an education, and there is no doubt concerning their honor and privilege in sharing the burdens and helping to make real the dreams of these citizens of the United States than whom there are none of finer original stock, or of greater staunch loyalty to the fundamental principles of citizenship. (Marion Francis, by Don Miller)

"When the 'weary mountaineer' reigned in his horse after his twelve-mile ride and told Miss Marsh and Miss Weston how he had come for help for his neighbors and told him to 'get with it' in matters of education. He opened the door of 'Singin Carr' to the great community urge of the twentieth century as well as a great door of opportunity to everyone who helps by even so much as a good wish, the builders of the school buildings among the pines close to where grandpop and friends are 'a-lyin.'" (By the editors of *The Farmer's Wife*)

The following was written by Marsh and Weston for *The Farmer's Wife*:

"One dusty, blistering, hot August in the mountains of Kentucky, a weary mountaineer urged his equally weary horse to the finish of a twelve-mile ride. He had come from Singin' Carr, as it is familiarly called, the struggling community of Dirk, Knott County, Kentucky. He had made a long ride to get something for which the heart of him was sore, a teacher.

"Two of us 'foreign' women—meaning women from 'outside,' beyond the mountains, where schools were good and teachers to be had—answered the call from 'Macedonia,' Ruth Weston and I.

"'We ain't a bit afraid,' said the caller from Singing Carr or Carr Creek, 'but what we can git a house for you to live in. If ye'll just come and help us get started. We're poor but I reckon they's enough food on Carr to feed ye.'

"The man who had come on this quest for help for the oncoming generation told us with a certain sort of patient eloquence, of the long, disappointing struggle. A year before, the little community had enthusiastically raised the frame of a schoolhouse. They had given the land and they gave the timber. The gift of 'timber' meant actual hard work, chopping and hauling; then they gave their labor and got the framework of the building up. And then came the bitter disappointment. Promises had been made that if they would give the land and timber—as they had—money would be supplied for the remainder of the materials and labor. The county, a poor one, had already given all that was in its power to give.

"The promised funds, because of sickness and its inevitable cost, failed to come. What were they to do? They had heard of Miss Weston and myself (Olive Marsh) and decided to make a bold appeal for help. So we came.

"Aunt Lucy, ninety years of age, was our first hostess. She is the oldest member of the Carr Creek Community and one of the most interested. She took us two 'foreign women' into her home for a month while we were waiting for the little cottage on the mountain side to be finished and for that month her home was the headquarters of the Community Center.

"The story of that cottage, which we have named The Patchwork Cottage, is why we stayed long enough to see it through its early struggles for survival.

"So it was through the generosity and 'advanced thought' of Aunt Lucy and others like her, so interested to have a school for the young mountaineers, that we finally were able to live in our Patchwork Cottage on the mountain side, about five rods from the peaceful spot 'where Pap is lyin'.

"Windows and parts of windows had been donated; old pieces of screen did their duty; the earnestness of the people to make it possible for a teacher to live among them, was such as to inspire and arouse the most laggard to utmost service.

"Before the Patchwork Cottage was finished—so to speak—Miss Weston began her primary teaching in an old storehouse that let in the rain and kept out the light. Mr. Hiram Taylor, a mountain storekeeper and teacher, began teaching the older children in a small and still less habitable room of the storehouse. The only light in this room comes through the door when it is open or through the chinks between the planks. The seats are rough boards nailed together.

There are no desks and there is a constant competition between the voices of the reciting children and Aunt Lucy's pigs who live not far off.

"Looking down from the mountain side upon this little, temporary school in its dark little hollow, stands the naked frame of the school building. I am looking at it as I write and I long for the help of some generous hand that will cover skeleton and equip the school for the faith of these mountaineers deserves to be met more than half way!

"The 'new school' around which clusters such fond hopes and dreams—and ninety year old Aunt Lucy ranks high among the dreamers—commands a wonderful view of the surrounding mountains and the bottom land through which Carr Creek goes singin' its world-old, wordless song.

"'I'm glad the school's up that-a-way,' said a mother of 12 children, 'for it's good for the chaps among the pines.' Just beyond the school there is a natural spring from which gushes pure, clean water, unpolluted with the vicious typhoid germ, the scourge of the bottom lands. This too will be 'right smart healthy for the school children.'

"Just beyond the unfinished schoolhouse in the pines is our Patchwork Cottage. In its tiny living room the primary school has 'its books.' The seats are just planks of wood resting on moveable blocks of woods.

"Through two windows we get 'light aplenty.' There are two other windows, boarded up temporarily, one with planks, the other with a door. Only the first plank floor has been laid and as it had to be made of unseasoned wood, the cracks grow steadily wider. On sunny days, we wrap up in whatever we can find and even have school out in the sunshine. But the children do not mind the cold. They have in them the sturdy spirit of their native pines and their truly wonderful ancestors. 'Cold or no cold, I'm a-comin' every day,' and Willard smiles intently into the teacher's face. 'There ain't no turning me!'

"Willard is one of nine children. The family lives in a typical two-room cabin. But they are sincerely seeking an education. It is a sight to see three of them riding to school on a ricky old mule, these snowy days. They have to cross Carr Creek in order to reach the Patchwork Cottage. 'And, it seems, to mule ears, the voice of Singin' Carr must have charms,' says Willard to teacher: 'Does you-all count it late if the mule stands in the middle of the creek an' there's no moving him? If it was that-a-way, I reckon you just wouldn't.'

"And I reckoned I wouldn't—and didn't.

"The mountain mothers are all hardworking. Wholeheartedly they want 'learning' for their children and somehow they find time and somehow they find cloth to put patch upon patch so that the children will be decently covered for school." (I remember.)

"The older women spin and knit. In many cases, the blankets have been made by the ancient handlooms. Miss Weston and I are going to try to revive this fine old industry, which has begun to die because women with families of from ten to fourteen children have little time for weaving. Aunt Lucy was one of the champion weavers of her day and she still wears a linsy woolsy skirt which, she tells us, she wove 'just after my last man went to the other war and never came back.' Its black-and-red checks are still bright and it is none the less warm for its huge patches.

"When our school building is habitable—may all good hearts help us speed the day—Miss Weston and I plan to have a room where we can set-up a loom and teach weaving to the young girls.

"Corn is the food staple. Unless it can be made to grow, there will be no food. All the members of each family must work in the corn fields, spring, summer, and fall. And the field is the steep mountain side, so steep that at first glance—and second and third—it seems impossible for even a mule to stand there and much less to plow. But it is done.

"On hot summer days, men, women, and children climb the mountain side, hoes over shoulders. To hoe in the upper row is an honor, so there are many contests and proud is the 'chap' who wins first.

"In the fall, the leaves are pulled from the corn stalk to be preciously hoarded for fodder. The corn in the ear is left on the stalk till it has been touched by the frost three or four times. This corn planted and cultivated and harvested by such hard work on the part of all, is food for pig, chicken, and folks. From the meal the women make the famous Kentucky corn bread and I defy anyone to prepare a more appetizing meal than Aunt Lucy does of fried chicken and corn bread." (Only my mother, Miss Marsh.)

"In spite of poverty and crowded, chilly cabins, the

people are happy and their religious spirit is deeper and more genuine than any I have met elsewhere. Every month, a "meeting" is held at the head of Carr. Everybody goes on Sunday, men and women riding double on mules; whole bunches of beautiful children astride ambling farm animals. The preachers wait for inspiration before they preach and it is miraculous what words come from the lips of several illiterate mountaineers.

"'Stuttering Johnny' will preach for an hour without the least sign of hesitation.

"And so, in spite of a chilly Patchwork Cottage, we two 'foreign women' are glad we answered the call of the weary horseman who rode twelve miles to deliver the Community appeal in person [Mr. Marion Francis]. We know that the people have done all they can. They have no money to buy materials and it is our work to get it for them. We know that the solution of the mountain problem lies in establishing these community centers. Through them, feuds will be erased and the moonshine still will be a thing of the past. If good men and women out in the world who have to spare of this world's good, will close their eyes for a moment, and see the mists and the grayness of the mountains, the swirling creeks, the muddy roads and the stone paths, and seeing, understand and love and help, because the spirit of love is in their hearts, then the Patchwork Cottage will disappear and in its place there will be a sturdy community cottage with real glass windows letting in the sunshine, doors that stay closed when the wind blows, a 'sure enough' floor, through which you can't lose a pencil. And a school—a real school—with desks and a blackboard and light and warmth and happiness and—a FUTURE!"

In March 1927, Miss Marsh and Miss Weston severed their connections with Carr Creek and moved to California. Miss Marsh was needed to care for an elderly aunt, and Miss Weston's health was failing. We should never forget these two wonderful women. Without their early help there may not have been a Carr Creek Community School. This brought another lady from Jersey Shore, Pennsylvania, Miss Margaret Humes, a graduate of Wellesley College in Boston, the daughter of a wealthy banker. Her D.A.R. background was one reason she came to Carr Creek to follow Miss Marsh, and Miss Weston was to keep Carr Creek afloat. She came for one year and spent 12 on the mountainside. She did that and more. She formed a D.A.R. chapter at Carr Creek; Campfire Girls and Boy Scouts; plus enlarged facilities for the orphan students. She loved the students and the community people.

Basketball was new to her, but she was truly proud of the 1928 basketball team, and she escorted them to Chicago where the team won three games in the National High School Basketball Tournament. She felt that these types of experiences were immeasurable for the educational growth of the students.

Thanks to Mrs. Dessie Amburgey for keeping a letter that Miss Humes had written on June 18, 1928, to raise money for Carr Creek. It is as follows:

Miss Jean M. Howat
State Treasurer, Ohio D.A.R.
Washington Courthouse, Ohio

My Dear Miss Howat:

We are very thankful to receive the contribution of $100.00 from the D.A.R. of the state of Ohio. Will you please convey our appreciation to those who have thus shown their interest in our work.

Our school year closed on May to reopen in August. The year just past has been a very busy, full one, in which we have realized some of our hopes for the people we serve. In November, through the kindness of President Hutchins of Berea, we conducted an Extension Opportunity School for the adults of our own and neighboring communities. Six of the staff at Berea College journeyed into our mountains for this new experiment on mountain education. Our high school of 42 attended each of the sessions. We had lectures on current topics of the day, Bible classes, agriculture, mother's meetings, chorus work, and games in which young and old joined. All the Berea people were delighted with the spirit of cooperation found "on Carr."

At Christmas we celebrated with our usual party for all, the giving of gifts and candy, special carol-singing at night all up and down the creek. A very impressive nativity play which is always a joy of our hearts, remembered all through the year. We also supplied Christmas cheer to 10 little district mountain schools, 700 children in all.

The pluck, skill and determination of these mountain lads gained for them, and for their kinds, the admiration of all lovers of clean, young manhood and fair play. Our basketball team has won tournament after tournament through hard battles on their part. And they were invited to the National Tourney in Chicago, as if fairy tales had come true indeed.

It has never been our aim, nor our purpose to promote athletics, we have merely permitted them as a part of the development of youth. Naturally, we are very proud of this new record, because it proves that mountain young folk can excel in a given undertaking if they have even half a chance. The boys were feted and lauded wherever they went, and their expenses paid either by friends or by exhibition games. In all, they conducted themselves as gentlemen, worthy of the name. The Kentucky State Y.M.C.A. awarded them the silver loving cup for the cleanest sportsmanship in the state!

In May, we graduated our second class from our newly accredited high school—three girls and five young men. A real commencement included the class play, "Abraham Lincoln," and baccalaureate and graduation addresses by speakers from Berea and DePaul University.

Next year we hope in every respect to "carry on" better than ever before, and for your help, we thank you deeply.

Very Truly Yours,
Margaret Humes

Epilogue

I had intended to end this book with the chapter "Lest We Forget"; however, new and very important information has developed that should be in included in the 1956 story.

Kentucky Educational Television (K.E.T.) was on the Carr Creek Hill Campus on Saturday, September 2, 2000, to record a segment of the Carr Creek basketball heritage, emphasizing the 1956 state champions. They took on a herculean task: to tape all the small schools that have won the Kentucky State Championship. K.E.T. felt that Carr Creek High, being the smallest school to ever win the state championship, was an excellent place to begin.

What an honor for this small school. I hope all the "Creekers" were grateful and impressed to be the first high school selected. The K.E.T. film crew, director, and producer were excited about the opportunity to be "Creekers" for a weekend, so to speak. They interviewed the champions and taped them after all the schools were taped. The documentary was aired on K.E.T. in 2002, and possibly on other public broadcasting stations. Thank you, Tom Thurman (director), Marilyn Meyers (producer), Michael Sollimer (videographer), and others, for honoring us. We are proud and humbled. May you remember your day on "the Hill."

We contacted all the players and cheerleaders by telephone, or wrote notes—no smoke signals—and we found excitable, grateful Creekers who were on the Hill for their first reunion in the old gym in decades. Bob Sheperd arrived from Texas early and stayed late—enjoying his teammates, cheerleaders, and, of course, the loyal fans.

Of the original ten players, eight were there! We have nine players left; John C. Mullins and his wife, also a Carr Creek graduate, were killed in an automobile accident while coming to the Carr Creek reunion in 1989. Forward Ray Stamper underwent major surgery and was home convalescing during the K.E.T. filming.

There was a Creeker reception with lots of party foods for the fans and their heroes on Saturday, September 2, 2000, on the Hill and the Old Indian Gathering Ground—where the Carr Creek Indians began their journey to the 1956 championship.

Index

Printed in the USA
CPSIA information can be obtained
at www.ICGtesting.com
JSHW082203140824
68134JS00014B/395

9 781596 528222